HEY YANG,

Where's My Thousand Bucks?

AND OTHER TRUE STORIES OF STAGGERING DEPTH

ANDREW YANG

AKASHIC
BOOKS
BROOKLYN, NEW YORK
Publishing books since 1997

Published by Akashic Books
©2026 Andrew Yang
All photographs courtesy of Andrew Yang

ISBN: 978-1-63614-279-1
Library of Congress Control Number: 2025941621
First printing

EU Authorized Representative details:
Easy Access System Europe
Mustamäe tee 50, 10621 Tallinn, Estonia
gpsr.request@easproject.com

Akashic Books
Brooklyn, New York
Instagram, X, Facebook: AkashicBooks
www.akashicbooks.com
info@akashicbooks.com

To everyone who has made "Andrew Yang" a thing.

Thank you.

Table of Contents

Introduction

"Hey Yang, where's my thousand bucks?" I've gotten that question dozens of times from people on the street, often in New York City. It's typically asked in a jovial, slightly challenging way. You see, I ran for president in 2020 on the promise of a "Freedom Dividend" of $1,000 a month for every American age eighteen or older, otherwise known as Universal Basic Income (UBI).

My response? "I'm working on it!" Followed by a fist pump or a wave.

Am I working on it? What does that even look like? Maybe I'm full of shit.

This book is my attempt to do a few things at once. First, it's to make you laugh. Or grin. Or reflect. This is a tough time, but that doesn't mean we can't smile and enjoy ourselves. It's actually probably going to help us do better if we can laugh a little. Some alternate subtitles for this book were *A Journal of Deep Thoughts* and *Reflections of Profound Profundity*. Will we get there? Maybe.

Second, it's an attempt to make a few points in a different way. I've tried a presidential campaign, three nonfiction books, a novel, endless social media posts, dozens of speeches, and hundreds of interviews to get a message out. But you know what works best? Humor. I'm hoping that this book reaches some people who have low interest in reading the news, especially lately, but want a good time—and maybe a few ideas will stick.

Third, it's a bit of therapy for me. A little self-indulgent, but I understand things better if I write them down. If I tell some of the stories from the past several years, perhaps we can enjoy them together and develop a better spirit.

Last, it's meant to share my journey with people who have cared and made it possible. "Andrew Yang" is only a thing because of you. What's been going on behind the scenes? Is there an actual person there? I hope you feel like this is something of a love letter and expression of gratitude.

Plus, some of the stories are pretty fun.

Am I serious? Only if I have to be. Let's Make Americans Totally Happy! It's the new #MATH, which stood for Make Americans Think Harder. Thinking harder didn't win the day, but maybe we can get there another way.

Part I

HOW IT STARTED

Chapter 1

"Do I know you?"

"**A**ndrew Yang! So what have you been up to?" This is another question I get a lot from perfect strangers on the street or in the airport. It's very hurtful. Don't you know all of the stuff I've been working on? Didn't you see my TED Talk?

I'm mainly kidding. But there's something funny about being a public figure whom people recognize walking out and about. It's generally happiness, but then a wonderment as to where you've been.

I get recognized on most any given day. Often, it's "Andrew Yang, love your work" or "Keep it up!" or "Run again, please!" Many young people ask, "Can I get a selfie?" I also get, "I follow you on Twitter/X/Instagram/TikTok!"

Sometimes there's a sense of familiarity without recognition. A middle-aged person will pause, squint, and ask, "Did we go to school together?" or, "Are you on CNBC?" Often someone will look at me and say, "Do I know you?"

I shrug and respond, "I'm on TV sometimes."

One time, a friendly young woman asked, "Excuse me, am I racist or are you Andrew Yang?"

I said, "I don't know the answer to the first one, but the answer to the second is . . . yes." It might have been funny to have said no and act offended.

When asked what I'm up to, I sometimes say, "Trying to make good things happen." And I've been working, even if it doesn't always get picked up in the media.

I'm a presidential candidate from a past cycle. There was a period when the energy around me was overpowering. I would get recognized *everywhere* I went. Almost half a million Americans donated to my presidential campaign—thank you, if you're one of them—and I received more individual donations than anyone in the history of New York City mayoral campaigns. I could barely go anywhere without people stopping and pointing.

I will say that I'm generally quite happy to be stopped and asked for a pic or selfie.

Back in 2017, my wife Evelyn asked me, "Do you think we'll lose our privacy?"

I laughed. "Would you recognize Amy O'Rourke on the street? Or Jeanette Rubio? We'll have nothing to worry about."

The celebrity was an aspect of a presidential campaign that was trying to get big things done. And I imagine I am still that person trying to get

big things done . . . but if I'm honest, I know it's
been awhile since 2020.

To my friends, I sometimes jokingly compare
myself to a rock band that had a massive album
five years ago. Maybe you saw me on tour. Haven't
you heard my new music? Of course, it's not really
an option for me to go around playing the old hits
in Iowa. That would be bizarre.

This is not a trip down sympathy lane. I never
set out to be famous. And the truth is, I've es-
chewed doing things that a lot of former candidates do to maintain a spotlight. I've turned down
media opportunities. I've gone out on my own. I
haven't succumbed to the mind-numbing incentives to burnish a profile. Heck, I turned down a
potential opportunity to be RFK Jr.'s running mate
as well as of course run myself, because I thought
it would do more harm than good. *Kennedy/Yang*
would have made a fun bumper sticker. But that's
not the goal.

Celebrity isn't an end, but a tool that I use, I
think, to try to make good things happen. Imagine
raising millions of dollars to fight poverty? I did
that.

And I sometimes get paid to show up to something. Like when Mike "The Situation" Sorrentino
gets paid to show up to a nightclub, but instead of
a nightclub it's a conference or a gathering of rich
people talking about artificial intelligence (AI) or
the future.

Imagine being yourself for a living. That's been my life for the last several years. I've been working hard. But sometimes even *I* wonder, *What exactly have I been doing?* Let's find out.

Chapter 2

Mr. Mayor

I can tell you what I did in 2021: I ran for mayor of New York City.

At first I was lukewarm on running—I thought it was something of a no-win job. Mayors of NYC seemed to lose their minds. And it wasn't the sort of environment where you could implement Universal Basic Income. I was wooed into the race by a number of political consultants who showed me polling in the lead. I warmed up to it when they told me the budget of New York City was about $100 billion a year. "Imagine the good you could do!" I figured I could improve the budget allocation and efficiency by at least 2 percent, or the equivalent of $2 billion a year for four years. Eight billion dollars of good! If you don't take on that kind of opportunity, what are you doing?

Plus, I had just concluded that the country needed a new approach to politics, and it would be pretty lame to make that argument and then turn down a major, winnable race. Got to walk the walk, not just talk the talk.

Last, I was severely underwhelmed by the candidates in the race. I thought, *These candidates are terrible. I would do a much better job than any of these jokers.*

And so it was that I announced my mayoral campaign on my forty-sixth birthday on January 13, 2021, with a slick video filmed by Darren Aronofsky of me walking the streets of New York in the cold. I ate pizza, played the piano, and greeted people. It was almost as good as *Black Swan*. That was a good night, as the video got hundreds of thousands of views in hours. It might have been the high point of the campaign.

The next day I showed up at an event in Harlem, and then-mayor Bill de Blasio leaned over and whispered in my ear, "Welcome to the zoo."

He wasn't kidding.

That race was not fun at all. It was COVID time in the winter and offices were still largely shut down. I was walking around campaigning and caught the kind of COVID that knocks you out for days. But I had to get up. Then I got kidney stones, which was perhaps the most miserable pain I've ever felt. I have a very high tolerance for pain, but I croaked to Evelyn that morning on my knees from the foot of the bed, "I think I need to go to the hospital." She piled me into a cab to the hospital twenty blocks away in Manhattan where our kids were born.

While I was lying in the hospital that day recovering, my phone blew up with well-wishes. Turns out my kidney stones made national news.

I got up the next morning, but in the coming days I wished I had simply stayed in bed. I was accused of hating animals, being corrupt, being a fool, belittling gay people because I said I loved them, being anti-women—you name it. A staffer wrote a tweet that resulted in social media venom for days. And Asians were getting attacked on the street during COVID.

I kidded with a staffer on a particularly bad day, "You should go out there and shove an old Asian lady to the ground. Make sure and say, *This is a hate crime!* while you do it. That will give us a news cycle."

There were any number of people with mental health issues on the street during that time. I personally broke up an attack on a photographer on the Staten Island Ferry. I was literally Batman. Didn't matter.

I will say, the assailant calmed down when he saw me. His eyes widened, he let out a "Yaaaaaannnng???" and lowered the pole he was using to attack the photographer. The same guy would go on to hospitalize an elderly man on the subway a few weeks later.

One time at an event in Harlem, a mentally ill Asian guy who was stalking the campaign started heckling me. "Andrew Yang, you suck!"

There was a black homeless guy on the corner deciding whether to pay attention or not. The Asian guy gave him a twenty-dollar bill and essentially enlisted him to start yelling the same thing. Now there were two of them yelling it: "Andrew Yang sucks! Andrew Yang sucks!" On one level, I thought it was hilarious. On the other hand, I was like, *I should probably keep it moving in case they find another homeless mentally ill guy and form a trio.* Everyone knows that three people equals a movement.

A friend came up from South Carolina to help the campaign and said, "Yo, these people are crazy, y'all."

One of the bright spots was greeting baseball fans on opening day at both Citi Field and Yankee Stadium. I stood outside and high-fived New Yorkers for an hour, taking selfies. "Hey, Andrew Yang, go for it!" In the Bronx, I was open about the fact that I was a Mets fan, and Yankees fans didn't care. I went in and took in part of the game both times. Those afternoons were a lot of fun.

Another high point was saying to Eric Adams during a debate, "You've achieved the rare trifecta of corruption investigations, and we all know it would be the exact same thing if you were mayor." That quote wound up pretty prescient. Eric Adams talked about how his favorite thing in his apartment was his bubble bath. Meanwhile, the apartment in Brooklyn that he showed reporters where he supposedly lived didn't even have a bathtub. I have a feeling his bubble bath was in New Jersey.

I consoled a cop's family and another grieving family during the campaign. Evelyn says that I dodged a bullet, that being mayor of New York is a job that eats people up. She's probably right. I'm sure I'd have been attacked for all sorts of things that happened the past four years, though I probably would have at least avoided being indicted. The insular NYC political machine got the better of me. I finished in fourth place despite leading in the polls for most of the campaign.

Losing stunk.

I think that people underappreciate what it means to run a campaign and lose. Now, I'd already lost a presidential campaign, but just about anyone would say that was a winning loss; we made seven presidential debates, activated millions of people, changed the national conversation about automation and AI, introduced UBI into the political landscape, and made #YangGang a movement. I outlasted seven congressmen, three senators, three governors, two mayors, one cabinet secretary, and three of Zach's girlfriends. (That's Zach Graumann, my campaign manager, who has been with me since 2018; he left a cozy job on Wall Street to try to abolish poverty. He's a great guy with a dark past. Kidding! His past is fine. He grew up in Connecticut and is a Bills fan.)

During the campaign, we gave away at least

$180,000 to fifteen different families. I traveled to Nevada right after we suspended the campaign to comfort crying volunteers. Even a good loss was emotional and exhausting.

A bad loss makes you feel like your life force has been drained in a way that's almost indescribable.

Someone called out to me on the street the other day, "Love you, Yang, but you should have been a little tougher during the mayoral race. Love you, though."

He's probably right. I figured I was the congenial positive figure and was up in the polls for most of the time, so a break from form might not have worked. But part of me wanted to punch back at people: "You think I'm not a New Yorker? I've got a 917 phone number. What do you have, a 646 or 347 or some bullshit? Fuck you."

Losing to a corrupt figure like Eric Adams made it even worse. That guy literally doctored fake photos to carry around in his wallet so he could tell dramatic stories about them.

After the mayoral campaign ended, I felt a weight on my soul. Like a cloak of negativity that I had a hard time shaking. So much of my work and outlook was based on the sense that people are generally good. I ran into a lot of stuff during the New York campaign that was just gross and nasty. Reporters calling to dig for dirt on my family. Death threats. Here I thought I was, trying to do the city a solid by stepping up and running for a difficult job, and I got pilloried for it. Equally painfully, some people close to me got punished. And supporters of mine no longer regarded me as the future. I had dinner with one backer later who seemed to blame me for making him look bad. I'm sure I made various missteps, but you'd think the general message would be, *Nice try, we'll get 'em next time*, instead of, *Why'd you make me look like a schmuck?*

I remember going for a jog that summer and feeling enveloped by a swarm of bees that followed every stride—but the bees were just dark thoughts. Dark thoughts about people, their perception of me as a loser, my relationships and standing in the world, the desire to give up, my earning potential, and more.

One reason why we see certain people run for office and then never hear from them again is that it's very hard to put yourself out there and then come away feeling like people don't like you or that you failed. Think Al Gore and his beard. And he won the popular vote! I know some other ex-candidates that are meaningfully scarred. And I get it. After the mayoral election, it felt like contempt and hostility awaited me on every street corner. I didn't want to show my face.

But for me, that wasn't really a choice. I had a book coming out in October of that year, a few months after the primary race ended. I had people relying on me and commitments to keep. So I had to buck up and get back out there.

I'm now grateful for that. I got to exorcise some of my fatigue and negativity by getting out and meeting with folks. I was also reminded that there was a lot of love—hundreds lined up for my first book event in New York City. Special thanks to anyone who showed up for the *Forward* book tour and said hello! It meant a lot. I don't think I let on how beaten up I felt, because you don't generally let it show if you can help it.

Let's say I didn't have any significant obligations. Would I have been out there making a case a few months later? Or would I still be in a cave— or on a yacht—licking my wounds? Who the heck knows. I can't afford a yacht, so in my case it would have been a kayak.

All of this said, people who see me on the street will often say, "Man, I wish you had won." And I give them a fist bump and respond, "Next time."

I was an unlikely figure to have run for mayor, maybe even more so than president. How the heck does that happen, and why did I do it?

Chapter 3

Life at Home

It's at least a little necessary to go into my background. Plus, some of it's funny.

I was born in 1975 in Schenectady, New York. My parents were immigrants from Taiwan who met in college. Dad was a physicist for GE. His specialty was making screens flatter; he would jump up and down on them. Kidding, he worked in a lab. He grew up on a peanut farm in southern Taiwan with no floor, so he's a bit of a roughneck. He spits a lot. He swam in the local pond and came back from college to do farmwork during the summers. He got out of Taiwan by doing well on a test and studying physics.

He hated the cold. So why was he in upstate New York? Because GE was the only place that would hire him. He wasn't getting offers because his PhD adviser wasn't a fan. But his adviser was away when GE was hiring. So they shrugged and made him an offer. He later moved to IBM a few hours south, in part to escape the cold.

Dad was a pro wrestling fan. We would watch WWE together, and he would narrate like the matches were real: *"Rabish Rick is too powerful for him. Look at that move. So devastating."* Even *I* knew that they were staged.

When I was twelve or so, Dad hit a deer with his Ford Escort. The deer was dead, but Dad thought that it was a waste of food, so he took the deer, tied it to the top of the car, and drove to a butcher to get it chopped up. I came home to a freezer of frozen venison. My dad never got the car repaired because he thought it was a waste of money, so the dented car was a permanent reminder. The deer didn't taste great.

Another time my mom had a couple friends over. Dad didn't want to socialize so he took off. He wasn't an attentive driver. That time he backed into my mom's friend's car in the driveway and then drove off without uttering a word. Later, Mom's friend had to come back in the house and say, "Excuse me, Nancy, but I think your husband rear-ended my car." My mom was mortified. It was the lamest hit-and-run ever. Insert Asian driving joke here.

When Dad wanted to take us for a treat, we'd head to McDonald's. We would pour out two large fries into a pile in the middle of the tray and snap them up while eating our McNuggets or Big Macs. What we didn't notice for quite a while was that Dad had a habit of tossing the end of the french fry he was eating back in the pile; I guess he didn't want to eat the part of the fry that he had touched. By the end of the meal there were a bunch of tiny fry ends that my brother and I unwittingly ate for years! When we realized what was happening, we were furious.

My mom is more or less an angel. She and Dad met at UC Berkeley, where she got a bachelor's in math and a master's in statistics. She's the glue to our family and the reason we talk to other people. She would shake her head every time she washed the dishes: "Hooo, when I was in college, my job was to wash test tubes in the lab. Your dad said if I married him, I would never wash dishes again. So what do I do every night? Wash dishes." She took us to piano lessons and Chinese school and tennis camp. By day she was the director of computer services at the local public university, SUNY Purchase. She gardens, arranges flowers, and is now an award-winning pastel artist. (Seriously, check out nancyyangart.com.)

I was a very quiet, nerdy, sensitive kid. I got named "Most Pensive" in preschool because I never talked. I read comic books and fantasy novels and played with action figures, *Star Wars* and G.I. Joe in particular. My older brother and I discovered Dungeons & Dragons and spent endless hours crafting characters and having adventures. My characters tended to take one of three forms:

the suicidal warrior, the scarred magic user, and the happy-go-lucky thief.

My parents didn't know what pajamas were. I went to sleep in whatever clothes I wore that day my entire childhood. It was only in middle school that I figured out that wasn't cool. I also regularly wore the same clothes multiple times a week, until another kid called me a "dirtbag" and I had to figure out what they were talking about.

There was a "country day" in my middle school where we all brought in food from our parents' culture. Most kids brought in pasta or Italian sausages. I brought in a rice cooker of fried rice. The other kids freaked out—"You eat this at home? Your house is like a Chinese restaurant?" I didn't tell them about the Vitasoy milk or bean curd in the fridge.

My town, Somers, was 96 percent white, with a high concentration of Italians. I suppose you'd call them "guidos" in politically incorrect eighties parlance. When *Platoon* came out in middle school, one of the kids kept standing next to me saying, "You see that? That's the way the gook laughs." I was one of the only Asian kids in town. There was one other Chinese girl and everyone said we should date. We both hated it.

I got reminded of my race quite often. Here are some of the more memorable samples:

"What's up, Chink?"

"Hey Yang, how's the wang?"

"Hey . . . you . . . wanna fight?" said with mouth moving but no sound coming out, to imitate a kung fu movie with bad dubbing.

"Ching chong, ching chong."

"Hey Yang, are you related to Long Duk Dong?"

"Hey, you know what Chinese use for blindfolds? Dental floss!"

"Hey Yang, you hungry? You want a gook-ie?"

"Hey Yang, I see where you're looking. No interracial dating."

"Hey Yang, what's it like having such a small dick? Everyone knows Chinese guys have small dicks. Do you need tweezers to jerk off?"

Middle-school kids are creative.

It didn't help that I had skipped a grade and was thus smaller and scrawnier than most of my classmates. I was the last kid picked in gym for most any team. I remember one day we were playing softball, and I got stuck in the outfield to minimize the chances of my getting involved in a play. Of course the ball got hit right to me. It was a pop fly, eminently catchable. It hung in the air for what felt like forever.

"Catch it! Catch it!"

I raised my glove to catch the ball. The sun hit my eyes. I squinted up. And . . .

The ball hit the heel of my glove and bounced out.

"Ahhhh! Throw it, throw it!"

The batter was sprinting around the basepaths. Another kid in the outfield who had come over grabbed the ball from the ground and threw it toward the infield. He then looked at me with a pained expression on his face and shook his head.

Here's a pic to give you an idea of what we were working with:

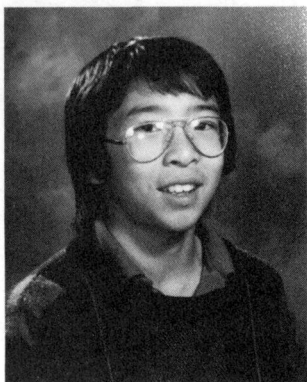

The braces were coming soon.

I had a few natural responses to the ridicule. I became quite self-conscious and alienated. I wondered if I did indeed have a small dick. There were many days I wanted to avoid school altogether.

Last, I became very, very angry.

Chapter 4
Growing Up Alien

My first job was as a busboy at a local Chinese restaurant, the Imperial Wok. I was a busboy because my written Chinese was too weak to translate customer orders for the kitchen. The patrons were regularly confused by my perfect English. I'd see classmates eating there with their parents. The waitstaff got fed the leftovers after dinner, which were not very good, typically animal body parts that weren't appealing to customers. I'd often just eat the unlimited hot and sour soup with some fried noodles and put it on top of white rice. Never got old.

At the end of the night, we would divvy up the cash and the other workers would get in a minibus and head back to Chinatown in New York City. I would go home just five minutes away.

The whole time, I got straight A's and was known as the smart kid. In junior high, I swept just about every academic award while trying to hide that fact from my peers. How to avoid being the nerd in town? I wrestled for a year to try to build up toughness. It wasn't a great fit; I was all arms and legs and pretty easy to pin. I had braces by then, and during one match my lips got cut on them despite the mouth guard. At least the blood made me look tough as I took the L.

I grew my hair out so that it covered part of my face and listened to the Smiths, the Cure, Depeche Mode, New Order, Nine Inch Nails, and other alternative bands. My first concert was Depeche Mode in 1989 on the *Violator* tour. One of my classmates mocked my T-shirt, calling it *Depress* Mode.

I took up skateboarding and wore oversized flannel shirts. I got my left ear pierced and put in a gold hoop earring and wore a bandanna. I got called "Aunt Jemima" and "Arr, matey" since I looked like a pirate. I seemed disaffected and gloomy enough that my school referred me to a therapist in ninth grade during my study period. She was a graduate student named Sue Denby— my first therapist!

I enjoyed therapy—it was fun talking about myself instead of chilling in study hall. After a semester or so, she said, "You know, I think you're fine." She gave me a hug on our last day. I think I was one of her first patients. I've recommended therapy ever since.

I accompanied the school chorus on piano. I also went out for the school play so I could go to

the cast party. I made the tennis team and modeled my game after Andre Agassi, with a lot less
power. If they returned my inside-out forehand, I
was sunk. (Total aside—Andre Agassi's biography,
Open, is one of the best sports bio books ever. Did
you know he was worried about his hairpiece falling off the whole time?)

I had a couple of friends. One was Miika, a
skinny music aficionado who would make mix-
tapes and wear colorful shirts. Miika's mom was
an immigrant from Finland. Miika would get me
into obscure bands like KMFDM ("Kill Mother
Fucking Depeche Mode") and Skinny Puppy. He
would drive us to the city or wherever for concerts
or a late-night diner for mozzarella sticks. He
would later become the bassist for a rock band in
Brooklyn while doubling as a designer for *Time*.

The other was Andy, my doubles partner on
the tennis team. Andy grew up all-American; his
parents met at Ohio State. His dad also worked
for IBM and his mom was a kindergarten teacher.
His mom baked chocolate chip cookies and apple
pie for any kids who came around. I would head
to Andy's house to play *Warcraft* or *StarCraft* or
whatever PC game was out. Andy had a ping-pong
table in his basement where we had many epic
battles.

As you can tell, there's nothing here that says
"future presidential/mayoral candidate," or even
"future anything." I wouldn't be chosen to be a

hall monitor and I would never think to run. I was more likely to be by myself reading science fiction or listening to mopey music than starting a school club. Years later, my mom would be asked, "How did you raise Andrew to run for president?" She would respond with some made-up bullshit about "letting him be himself." Kidding—love you, Mom!

I developed an affinity for underdogs from this period that would last most of my life. I became a Mets fan. I would find whoever was left out at a party and try to bond with them. I was dubious of groups, sometimes in an obnoxious way. I would, for example, later call fraternities "homes for the weak of spirit." I felt like an outsider. After all, if someone is going to be dubious of group dynamics, it would be the kid always on the outside looking in.

Chapter 5
Dead Poets Society

I was uncomfortable in my town, and asked my parents if they thought going away to boarding school would be a good idea. I got the idea from a girl I went to summer academic camp with. Yes, I took classes during the summers—I am Asian after all. My mom loved the idea, and I went to Phillips Exeter Academy in New Hampshire.

A lot of my motivation was that I was a fifteen-year-old junior in high school and my brother was leaving for college at UC Berkeley. I didn't want to be the only kid in my school who couldn't drive. Better to go away.

Here's me after arriving in New Hampshire in 1990:

Layers, lots of layers.

Exeter was intense. Some people regard it as the most competitive, pressure-cooker high school in the country. Mark Zuckerberg is probably the most famous alum, though he'd come years after me. The school recruited star athletes for every sport. One guy from my graduating class, Brandon Williams, would win an NBA Championship with the San Antonio Spurs seven years later. Most ordinary kids from public schools couldn't make a sports team at Exeter because they brought in ringers to make the teams awesome, including older kids who had technically already graduated from high school. There were men walking around among us boys.

One year behind me was John Forté, who would go on to produce the Fugees. He produced musicals for the high school assembly that were among the dopest things I've ever seen to this day. John was convicted of drug trafficking and served seven years before getting pardoned by George W. Bush. I meant to visit him in jail but never did.

One of my dormmates, Ed Ko, would go on to murder his ex-girlfriend and serve twenty-five years to life in prison. He's still locked up now. I played club tennis with Ed and he was always very quiet. Yes, the quiet, murderous Asian guy down the hall would go on to kill one of my schoolmates six years after we graduated. He's two guys to the left of me in this dorm picture:

Exeter produced extremes: pop stars, murderers, NBA champions, and a presidential candidate who would come back years later and ask the locals for their votes. Also, investment bankers. Lots and lots of investment bankers.

The school had a system where you had to contribute in every class to do well, so you became accustomed to presenting your thoughts every period. You were pretty much forced to talk if you wanted an A.

I wound up with the drama crew; I played King Herod in *Jesus Christ Superstar* and sang my way through a solo. I also joined the debate team and did so well that I was named to the US national team in 1992 and was sent to the World Public Speaking and Debating Championships in London. Yes, I was technically a high-level debater, though we got blown out by our hosts with their fancy British accents.

I asked a girl to the prom but she wouldn't go

with me because her parents didn't like Asians. I'm kidding, Hasan Minhaj–style! My prom date was a cute girl from Switzerland, Chloe, with whom I was buddies.

I finished near the top of my class and got into Stanford and Brown, choosing Brown because the Stanford climate seemed too sunny. Who studies in the sun?

I came out of Exeter with a newfound sense that the top kids in the country were no better than me. Okay, they were a *lot* better at basketball and music. And one of them was better at murder. But I could think and talk as well as any of them. It's not like that's a job, though—maybe lawyer? I still think of New England as a place where you go to grow up and learn among the winter and the woods.

Chapter 6

"Do you know karate?"

I got asked "Do you know karate?" hundreds, maybe thousands of times, as a kid.

The answer was no, but I would pretend. I loved kung fu movies like *Five Deadly Venoms* and imitated them. I bought ninja throwing stars in the city that I would launch at trees in the backyard. I bought plastic nunchuks and practiced with them. One time, I brought a butterfly knife I had bought in Chinatown to school. When I showed it to other kids, they were like, "Yo, that's real?" and got the heck away from me in case they'd get in trouble. I trained myself to be able to open and close the butterfly knife in rapid, threatening fashion. Yes, I was *that* kid.

When I was in college, I joined the tae kwon do club. Finally, I would become a badass. The teacher was a small Korean guy, Master Han, who managed several schools in Rhode Island and drove a sports car. One day he walked around the classroom with a closed fist and asked, "What is in my hand?" We started guessing:

"Anger."

"My chi."

"Power."

He shook his head and got to me.

"Nothing," I guessed.

He smiled and shook his head. "No. The universe is in my hand." He seemed very pleased with himself.

I studied tae kwon do for the first three years of college and eventually became a blue belt with a red stripe, which was somewhere in the middle. I looked the part—I was a six-foot-tall Asian guy with floppy hair who yelled loud. But I was a mediocre martial artist. On the way to one tae kwon do competition at Cornell, my cologne spilled onto my uniform and I walked around reeking of Claiborne for Men all weekend. My teammates noticed and started saying things like, "He smells too sexy to hit!" My opponents disagreed.

I joked with my teammates about moving to the middle of nowhere in the Midwest and opening Master Yang's Den of Death Dealing, where I would teach the locals various lethal techniques that I would make up. And when someone would ask me, "Master Yang, can you demonstrate the technique for us?" I would say serenely, "No. You must learn it for yourself." Eventually, I would be discovered as a fraud and run out of town.

I have been tired at various points in my life, but never have I felt so drained as I did between rounds at my first tae kwon do tournament. There's nothing quite like an adrenaline dump when someone is there to hit you in the face. You get filled with energy during the fight, yelling, and then you crash while you're sitting on the bench being coached. I remember getting up from the bench thinking to myself, *Just look like you're fine until the match is over.*

I broke wooden boards with a backspin hook kick and a jumping side kick and a bunch of other techniques during tests, but that's a lot easier than it sounds. One time, I asked to break a board with a ridge hand, kind of a reverse karate chop. I had seen the hero break boards with this technique in one of my favorite movies, *Best of the Best.*

"What technique are you using?" Master Han asked.

"Ridge hand, sir!"

Master Han furrowed his brow. "No. Jumping back kick."

"Sir, I have always dreamed of breaking a board with a ridge hand, sir!" I responded in true *Best of the Best* fashion.

He squinted at me and took my hand by the flesh between my thumb and index finger. "Use this part of your hand."

"Sir, yes sir!"

A few minutes later, I inhaled and exhaled deeply and slowly and guided my hand against a board of one-inch pine, mimicking the path of my strike. After two phantom pantomimes complete with dramatic exhales, I then yelled out, "Ah-huh!" and swung my hand forward as fast and hard as I could. The board broke with a loud *CRACK*. The crowd, mainly other students who were testing, applauded. But my hand immediately began throbbing, starting with the top knuckle of my index finger. I masked the pain while I took my place back in formation.

Then I felt my hand swelling up. After a few seconds, I said to Master Han, who was walking by my station, "Sir, permission to ice my hand, sir!" He waved me away in disgust. I put some ice in a cup and crammed my hand in it and returned to my place in line. My hand still throbbed, but I had accomplished a small dream.

Tae kwon do didn't go with me far beyond college. But the gym did.

Chapter 7

Pass the Protein

"**F**uck you."
"You're a loser."
"You suck."
"What's the matter with you?"

I would hear these things all the time. From my mom. Kidding! But the speaker was me, and the voice was in my head. This was my internal dialogue from my teens onward. I would berate myself regularly about nearly everything. If I had done something embarrassing or humiliating at school, I would replay it in my mind over and over again on a loop.

You remember how I said I was angry as a kid? It got worse in adolescence, with testosterone and peer pressure. The anger had to go somewhere.

The summer before college, I started going to the gym. I went with Andy, my old tennis doubles partner. At first I felt very self-conscious heading to our local health club. Many of the guys who were on the machines or in the weight room were old and huge. Guidos like to work out. It was daunting. But you have to start somewhere. I struggled for the first four weeks while Andy and I encouraged each other. It was addictive seeing my wiry muscles develop. By the end of that first summer, I could bench-press 135 pounds, which is something of a litmus test of manhood, because you start with the big plates and don't have to change them every time.

I hit the gym at Brown with gusto. It became part of my identity. When my college girlfriend left me for another guy, I took it very hard. It got even worse when I totaled my Honda Accord on the way to Boston one rainy night trying to get away from campus. That felt like a real low—I rear-ended the car in front of me on the highway. Thankfully no one was hurt.

Just about the only thing I could do that helped me get through the days was work out. It became a constant companion and haven. Chest and biceps one day, back and triceps another day, and then the worst day of all—legs and shoulders.

Have you ever gone to the gym and seen an angry Asian guy? That was me for a period of years, always trying to shake the disease. I would lie prone on the bench, listen to rappers like Nas and Fabolous on headphones, and curse to myself while maxing out.

By the time I was out of college, I could bench-press 225 pounds eight times in a row. Here are a couple pics that give you a sense of it, including my driver's-license photo from when I was twenty-one:

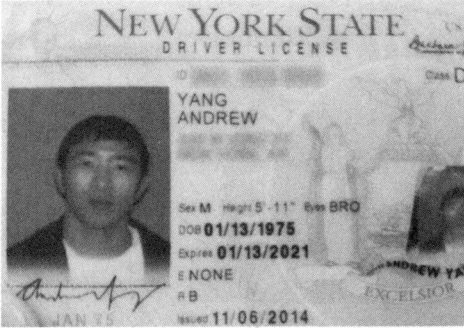

Note the thick neck.

What a Chad.

At one point while I was washing my clothes in a communal laundry room, a woman who I didn't know saw me walking around in a tank top and commented to her friend, "What a meathead."

It was a thrill. I had been trying to escape being the Asian nerd for years. Had I made it?

Nah, the voice inside you isn't that easy to shake. The best one can do is mute it a little bit temporarily, make it less overwhelming. Hungry? Drink a protein shake. The only decent flavor is chocolate, it masks the taste.

So, muscles. What to do with them?

Chapter 8
Hoop Dreams

Basketball has played a big part in my life. It's up there with Prince. (Underrated Prince song—"Forever in My Life.") I loved hoops from early on.

This is not to say that I was good. Once, when I was around ten years old, I was playing with a bunch of kids at school. I blew a wide-open layup. Why was I so open? Because people weren't worried about guarding me. One kid said, "Hey, I guess that's a Chinese layup!" and the other kids laughed. I was small, skinny, and didn't have a sense of what I was supposed to do on the court. I went out for the JV team my first year in high school and got cut. Since I had skipped a grade, I was always physically behind.

Still, I loved to play. I would shoot for hours by myself or with my brother in the driveway as the sun went down. I was transfixed by the battles Michael Jordan had with the Patrick Ewing–led Knicks in 1992 and 1993. All the kids in town were rooting hard for the Knicks, who were hard-nosed and rugged. John Starks's dunk on the Bulls in the Garden is still emblazoned in my mind all these years later. I began to obsessively follow the Knicks and the league, tracking the statistical leaders and the best potential draft picks.

It would be totally humiliating if I was a hoops junkie who couldn't play, so I decided to get better. I joined pickup games at my local park in the suburbs and in the school gym. At first, it wasn't great. I was a lot more comfortable playing half-court than full court; hours of one-on-one or two-on-two in a driveway will do that. But over time I got stronger and more skilled. I reached the point where I could play in most pickup games and be a quality add—it helps that I like to pass the ball. After college, I joined a run with a group of fifteen guys who rented a gym on Saturdays and played every weekend. I also played outdoors at the local park on the west side of Manhattan on weeknights.

If I had to compare my game to someone at that time, it was a much smaller Grant Hill. I had a sneaky right-to-left crossover dribble that enabled me to get a step on most defenders. I had a good if somewhat streaky midrange jump shot; I would use the glass a lot from the corners, Tim Duncan style. And I had a back-to-the-basket postgame where I could hit a turnaround jumper going either direction, modeled loosely after Larry

Johnson; I was in the Garden when L.J. hit the four-point play for the Knicks in the '99 playoffs.

During this time, I became a truly obsessive Knicks fan. Latrell Sprewell was a hero to me. So what if he'd choked his coach? I'm sure the coach said something to deserve it. I felt how the Knicks did was a metaphor for my life. It helped that they would make at least the second round of the playoffs for eight straight years, from 1992 to 2000. Not coincidentally, I detested Michael Jordan and the Bulls, though now I acknowledge that he's the GOAT and I miss him.

Playing basketball was like therapy. Have a shitty week at work? Forget about it on the court. That woman never call you back? Go get a run in. Some of my fondest memories from my twenties involve sweating on a sunny blacktop with friends.

One summer morning in Battery Park, I got there before my buddies and was shooting alone. A couple joggers ran by. A lanky white guy in basketball shorts and a hoodie showed up and asked, "Hey, can I shoot around with you?" He had a floppy haircut; he looked familiar.

Then it dawned on me, and my eyes widened. "Holy shit, you're Steve Nash!" He had just won the NBA MVP award a couple months earlier. "Sure!" I was living a Nike commercial.

Steve proceeded to shoot around, but they weren't normal shots. He would take two steps and lean back to shoot off one foot or the other, as if a bunch of giant bodies and arms were reaching for him. After a few shots, he switched to rebounding for me. I thought that was obscene—Steve Nash rebounding for my off-target jump shots? I proceeded to clank every shot because I was so amped up. I thought, *Screw it*, and switched back to rebounding for him. Several minutes later, a couple of my buddies showed up, so Steve said "Thanks" and left. I went to my friends: "That's fucking Steve Nash!"

One of them was like, "No way." Another glanced over at the departing Steve and said, "Holy shit, that *is* him!" I was glad he could confirm my story. Steve was like a basketball hipster ghost, gone as silently as he'd arrived.

Another time at the same court, we were playing three-on-three with a couple of strangers. One was a middle-aged black guy in a tank top. He took to barking at his teammates, including a friend of mine who was a smaller Asian guy. "Yo, don't take that shot!" "Yo, man, learn how to play!" He was obnoxious.

I looked at him and said, "Man, shut the fuck up and play ball."

He immediately stopped and came up to me, eye-to-eye. We were the same size: "What did you say?"

I wasn't particularly afraid because I had a bunch of friends around and he was alone. Plus, I was annoyed. I looked him dead in the eye. "I said, SHUT THE FUCK UP AND PLAY BALL."

He backed away and I figured that was the end of it. But the next time I got the ball, I felt a knee in my back. He had done a jumping Macho Man Randy Savage high knee into the middle of my back. I sprawled to the ground, scraping my knee and hands as the ball skittered out of bounds. Looking down, with the warm blacktop beneath my palms, I thought to myself, *All right, now I'm going to fight this guy.* And I felt pretty good about it. I was going to tae-kwon-do his ass.

I pushed myself up and turned to what I thought was going to be a confrontation, but he was halfway off the court, picking up his things and leaving. My knee was bleeding a tiny bit. I was tense and pissed, but not so much that I was going after him. I stood in place watching him slink away.

My friends were like, "Are you all right? What an asshole." The one he had been riding the hardest seemed particularly happy to see him go. I sometimes imagine what would have happened if he had stayed to fight. My friends were lawyers and such, and not exactly prone to brawls. But still, there were four or five of us. And regardless, I was ready to pound the guy.

Another summer afternoon, I invited a friend along who was a better athlete than the rest of us. He was maybe six three and had played a bit in college. At one point, he drove the lane and it was me under the basket. I thought, *I'll try to challenge his shot*, and jumped, trying to get my hand up to the ball. We collided in the air. His knee went into my side and my hip erupted in pain. I flew back like I had been shot out of a cannon. I couldn't breathe. I lay on the ground for a minute with the wind knocked out of me. One friend hovered over me with concern while the game kept going.

Eventually, I was able to breathe and get up. I wound up with a giant, purple, splotchy bruise over my left hip and was done for the day. It made me realize that playing with a genuine athlete was a totally different animal than playing with my usual crew, and I should have just let him cram it. He'd made the layup anyway, despite me sacrificing my body.

As we got older, people started dropping out of the game for a variety of reasons: maybe they moved away or changed jobs; some were burdened with nagging injuries. I've lost touch with the guys I played with in those days, but I still think of them affectionately. I wonder if any of them saw me on TV years later and said to their wife or partner, "I used to play basketball with that guy!" The truth is, I didn't even know most of their last names. That's what happens when you play ball. The game connects you.

Chapter 9

Swinging and Missing

Okay, I've been talking a lot about my spare time. What the heck was I doing for work and money in my twenties? Good question. After law school, I was a lawyer at a big corporate firm, Davis Polk & Wardwell. Pretty soon, I had two thoughts:

1. I am getting better at this job.
2. I hate this job.

I went home for Thanksgiving to my parents that November and said, "You did not come to this country for me to do this. It's mind-numbing." My job at the time involved scouring hundreds of pages of documents looking for issues.

"What are you talking about, Andy? You have a great job. We are very proud of you." Ah, Mom.

"You shouldn't be." I joked with my brother that when we were kids, I dreamed of going into the woods and killing a dragon, not being the fucking scribe.

So why was I doing this lawyer job? Aside from the fact that I'd spent three years in school for it, it had to be the money.

I've had something of a funny relationship with money. I guess we all do. My parents were suck-the-meat-out-of-the-bones stingy. My dad still takes joy out of getting through a day without spending a dime because he's found some free source of food.

When I was a kid, my mom used to tell me how much everything cost so we would know what she was spending on my brother and me. "You know how much *this* costs? You know how much *that* costs?" When I was a teen, I got fed up and said, "How about this, Mom: you can document everything you ever spend on me, and then when I'm older I'll repay every penny, and then we can never talk to each other again."

She was hurt. "Why are you so mean?"

"Okay, then if you're doing it out of love, stop talking about it."

Anyway, I've had a sense that I was going to need to work for money since I was a kid. As a teen I sold knives door-to-door—Cutco—and still remember the sales patter. Did I slice my hand with one of the ultra-sharp knives while cutting a bagel? Yes, I did. Those things were a menace.

I worked at the school library at Exeter for $6.25 an hour. I was a snack-bar employee frying chicken fingers at Josiah's during my first year at Brown. It was interesting how classmates wouldn't recognize you as soon as you put on a fast-food hat and apron. I was a camp counselor during the summers.

Looking back, this was probably a little bit excessive. I was a middle-class kid. My parents at one point told me to work less and study more. But I always wanted to make my own money. I was on a partial scholarship to Brown from IBM, but my parents often reminded me that they'd taken out a second mortgage on the house.

This extended past college into law school. In my second year, I got a summer associate job at a big firm. We were given a lunchtime reimbursement of fifty dollars if we ate with a current lawyer. I know, it's a lot of money, and everyone used it to eat at fancy restaurants. One time I went to lunch with a couple of associates and they picked a fairly normal restaurant. The lunch entrees were "only" seventeen dollars each, so I ordered two of them. Everyone at the table was like, "What are you doing?"

Embarrassed, I said, "Oh, I'm just really hungry," when the truth was that I just wanted to make sure and spend all fifty dollars. Who wants to leave money on the table?

I sensed everyone's eyes on me. I had to eat two lunches to avoid making it a thing. I moved the items around the dish to make it look done by hiding some remaining food under mashed potatoes.

After law school I owed $110,000 in student loans. The firm I joined paid $120,000 plus a bonus of $45,000 to start. It seemed like an absurd amount of money to pay a twenty-four-year-old who hadn't done anything and didn't know anything. It was more than my dad made, and he had generated sixty-nine patents for GE and IBM. I felt like I was way too young to be making that kind of money, but also that I shouldn't feel too committed. I didn't have kids, a mortgage, or even a girlfriend. Whose dreams was I supporting?

So I left the firm after five months to try to start a dot-com company. Stargiving.com would raise money for nonprofits, where if you clicked on an ad you'd help the charity and then maybe meet the celebrity. My parents thought I was a moron walking away from a six-figure job for my long-shot little start-up. Turns out they were right, as we would throw in the towel about a year and a half later.

I felt like a failure, lying on the floor of my little bedroom; I had moved in with Andy to save money and was paying $1,080 a month. I had gone through my savings. My classmates were still making six figures practicing law. I had a net worth of negative $100,000. But I wanted to get better at becoming an entrepreneur.

I got a job at a mobile software company that ran out of money a few months later. One of my colleagues moved into the conference room with duffel bags of his stuff and was showering in the office. "You're living the dream!" I said to him, trying to be positive. He glared at me. I found another job working at a software company that made health records digital.

Given that by then I'd been part of two companies that had gone under, I started looking for side hustles. I tutored students in standardized tests. I also began promoting parties under the name "Ignition NYC." We would host big parties in Tribeca.

These parties started with a simple but compelling question. A friend of mine asked me one night as we shared tales of rejection, "How do we become cooler?"

I answered, "We throw parties."

He said, "We can't do that, we live in tiny apartments with roommates. That won't look cool."

I said, "Then we use a lounge or bar. If we get enough people, they'll let us use it for free."

The reality was even better: if you got enough people to show up, the venue would actually pay you a percentage of the bar and give you some drink tickets. You could throw a big party and give free drinks to your friends and even make some money if you could get a couple hundred people to show up.

That didn't seem too hard for a twenty-six-year-old in New York City. I enlisted a few partners. One was Mike Skinner, Miika's roommate in Brooklyn who was also the drummer for his band.

Mike was a good guy. Another was Amy Engelhardt, who had grown up in the town next door; everyone had a crush on her. The last was Gunny Scarfo, our resident tech guy.

If you want to become an entrepreneur, it turns out throwing parties is a great way to start. We had some phenomenal parties, including one that drew five hundred people on New Year's Eve in 2003. Everyone was desperate for something good to do on New Year's Eve, which is a holiday everyone secretly hates. Sort of like Valentine's Day.

I had three jobs for about four years: healthcare start-up guy, tutor, and nightclub promoter. I was single for just about all of these years. One problem for me on dates was that I was very frugal. I lived on protein shakes and yogurt, so it was tough for me to switch gears and treat a woman to a nice meal. *Look on the inside and believe in me, ladies!* When I liked a woman who wasn't interested in me, I thought it was because I wasn't successful enough. Meanwhile, it was probably just me being insecure or a cheapskate.

Did I mention that I still owed six figures in law school loans? I started calling my loans "my mistress" because it felt like I was sending checks to support a phantom family in another town. I hoped they were living a good life.

Part II

LUCKY BREAKS

Chapter 10

An Overnight Success after Ten Years

Reading this, you might be like, *Wait, the parties sound cool. But how did this guy wind up running for president again?*

When I was thirty I became the head of the little education company, Manhattan Prep, that I was tutoring for. I guess I was pretty good, as I wound up the CEO.

I turned down the job at first. Being a tutor was the kind of thing you did as a summer job before moving on to your corporate gig. And in my case, it was a side hustle to fuel my entrepreneurial dreams. When I met someone at a party, I told them I worked at a healthcare start-up. That could mean anything. We had fancy investors. If I said I was working at an anonymous education company, it might seem sort of lame by comparison.

But I sensed a good opportunity, as the curriculum was excellent and the teachers were stellar. I thought I could make the company grow. I rolled up my sleeves and became the new CEO. I said to myself, *You HAVE to make this work.* I'd had multiple failures up to that point, like the Buffalo Bills, or the Knicks in the nineties. My parents weren't exactly broadcasting my professional exploits to their friends. They just told them I was still a lawyer.

Being CEO of a no-name education company was liberating in that I could just focus on growing a small business one student at a time. There was no more scrambling for new investors or hospital clients. My life became a lot simpler. It was: build a great team, establish a positive culture, do right by the students, and help them achieve their goals. Day in, day out.

We had some fun. I loved to hire whippersnappers who were up on the latest web trends. We taught courses online, built a web product, and invested in our social media. I also made sure we were #1 in the industry in teacher compensation and treating people well, including health insurance for anyone who was employed over half-time.

It worked. About four years later, we became #1 in the country in our category of preparing students for the GMAT, the test to get into business school. We ended up selling the company for millions of dollars to Kaplan. Because I was a part owner, I became a millionaire at age thirty-four. Also around this time, my parents started telling their friends I was smart again.

I know, how the heck does that happen? I'm an incredibly lucky guy. I then proceeded to squander it all on a yellow Lamborghini, the vehicle of my dreams. Nah, that's not my style. I can't even spell Lamborghini without an editor. The biggest indulgence I allowed myself was a suite at a Knicks game, to which I invited a bunch of friends, and an all-you-can-eat Brazilian meal at a nearby *churrascaria* with meat skewers that made it feel like a medieval feast.

Because of my frugal habits up to that point, I felt like my windfall was all the money in the world. I paid off my loans. I could do anything I wanted. I was rich. What would you do if money didn't matter?

I figured I'd spent the last six years training future bankers and consultants, which was not great. So then I'd spend the next six years training an army of entrepreneurs to fan out to Detroit, Cleveland, Baltimore, New Orleans, Providence, Birmingham, Philadelphia—to create jobs and become better people. I started an entrepreneurship nonprofit called Venture for America, donating $120,000 to kickstart the org.

Over the next number of months, I raised a couple million dollars for Venture for America. This was a real trip. Not only did I have some money, but it turned out I could raise enough money to pay myself a salary and do something wholesome I believed in—training young people to start and build businesses in parts of the country that could use a boost. I believed then, and still do, that entrepreneurship can bring out the best in people. The best entrepreneurs were folks who solved a problem that mattered to them. Imagine being in a position to give more people the chance to do things they care about in a way that will generate value and create jobs. What a privilege! What a country.

I ran Venture for America for six years as the founder and CEO. It wasn't that I was doing a job for money. I was doing what I thought was right, and if I believed in it enough, other people would too.

Chapter 11

The Secret

You know the secret to a highly readable book? Short chapters.

Chapter 12

Evelyn

Ah yes, the love of my life! I have already referenced my poor luck with women, which was a defining aspect of my twenties. I probably spent a grand total of one out of those ten years in what would be called a relationship. So if that's you too, don't give up hope, it can turn around fast.

I was thirty-one when Evelyn entered my life. We were introduced at an alumni event held on the campus of Columbia University. She was twenty-four; we joke now that I was a cradle robber.

When Evelyn and I first met, it wasn't a sure thing. Evelyn cut things off with me after a few dates, saying, "You're too intense for me, I just came out of a long-term relationship."

I felt this deep pain; I really liked her. So I steeled myself, drawing on years of experience of having things not work out. I had become comfortable with the ache. I wrote her a sincere email: *You're great, I totally think you should go out and experience things and not be tied down.* I came home from work that day ready for a night alone with some Chinese takeout, when my cell phone rang. It was Evelyn. I was very surprised—hadn't she essentially broken things off with me earlier that week?

"Hey, what are you doing?" she asked.

"Nothing," I replied.

"You want to come out to drinks with me and my friends from work?" Evelyn worked in marketing at L'Oréal. We would later find out that she was making more money than I was at the time, even though she was seven years younger. What can I say, my little education company wasn't *that* flush with cash.

"Sure," I said.

I went out and had drinks with her and her friend Chandni, who would be Evelyn's maid of honor at our wedding four and a half years later. I then went home alone, wondering if I would ever hear from her again.

But I did. She asked me to join her and her friends out a couple more times. She told me later that my note made her feel like I genuinely wanted what was best for her, even if I wasn't going to be in the picture—which was true.

About a week later she asked, "Why don't you ever call me?"

I responded, "Well, you kind of ended things with me, so I don't want to overstep."

"You can call me," she said.

And with that, we started dating. She moved in a little while later. I don't think it's any coincidence that my love life flourished at the same time I found a job that I could feel good about and committed to long-term. A lot of guys need to be settled professionally in order to be any good in a relationship. Many of us are sort of simple that way. It's one reason I feel sad about what's going on out there in the world: if you have fewer stable careers, you're going to have fewer healthy relationships.

Several years later, I decided to propose to Evelyn. I resolved that I was going to surprise her. Couples that talked it out ahead of time always seemed kind of lame to me—where was the romance? I bought Evelyn a ring and planned a trip to propose to her on the beach in the Caribbean.

I would make a lousy spy, because I feared she was going to see the ring the entire trip. I tried to play it cool but felt like a transparent mess. When the time felt right to me, we headed out on the beach and walked for about ten minutes. Finally, I went down on one knee, opened the little box to show her the ring, and asked her, "Will you marry me?"

Her response was the five words every person wants to hear while in that position: "Why are you doing this?" Apparently, Evelyn had not really considered the possibility that we should get engaged. I possibly did *too* good a job of surprising her.

I responded, "Well, we've been together for three years. We love each other. I want to start a family with you. I think we should get married."

The shock subsided from her face. "I think so too," she said. A "yes" followed a few seconds later. We hugged and kissed and started making wedding plans right there on the beach. We shopped around for a new ring afterward, and she decided she liked the one I got her the best. What are the odds?

We've now been married fifteen years and counting, and they've been the best years of my life. Thank you, Evelyn, for saying yes . . . eventually.

Chapter 13
The Two Lists

When I was in my twenties, I read an article about Ted Leonsis, who owns the Washington Wizards, as well as several other DC sports teams. He said that in his twenties he had written down a list of his life's goals, and one of them was, *Own an NBA team*. And then it happened. I was like, *What are the odds of that? That seems impossible*. So I decided to write my list down too.

Some of them were pretty straightforward and achievable:

Get married
Have two happy, healthy kids
Be a good son
Stay physically fit and active

Things that were pretty normal.
Some of them were kind of frivolous:

Go skydiving

Get season tickets to an NBA team
Own a dog

There were a couple of financial goals:

Own a home
Have enough money so you don't feel tied down

My standards weren't mega-millions high. My goals were more about impact than money. Some of them were wildly ambitious:

Build a successful company
Elevate one national political figure
Improve the lives of millions of people

Evelyn saw this list when we were dating and thought it meant I had some direction in life. I didn't imagine I'd head into politics myself. I am Asian, after all. I can prove without a shadow of a doubt that I wasn't thinking about politics as late as 2016; Venture for America operated in twelve cities and none of them were in Iowa or New Hampshire or South Carolina. I got into politics after Donald Trump won the presidency in 2016.

So that's the first list—what do you want to accomplish in life? Writing down your goals will lead you to move toward them, like magic. They could be small and achievable, like *Do twenty-five push-ups* or *Learn to cook a good pasta dish.* Or they could be big.

Every once in a while, you'll be presented with a choice to do something and you say to yourself, *I'd better do it, because it's on my list of goals. If not now, when?*

A lot of it will happen without you even noticing. You'll take action toward them automatically. I've achieved most of my goals, even the somewhat unrealistic ones. What have I not done? I'll come back to that.

The second list might be more important than the first.

In my thirties, I read a study that said that if you make a list of things you're grateful for, it will make you happier. You can refer to it every day and try to add something. Some can be very small, like *I'm grateful that today's a sunny day* or *I'm grateful for my local pizza joint.*

So I made my Gratitude List as a note on my phone. I refer to it anytime I need a pick-me-up. I try to do it every day. What's on it? Mostly people:

*My mom and dad are still healthy and up
and about
Evelyn
Christopher
Damian
My brother and brother-in-law*

But it also gets kind of small and random:

My favorite bakery (I've got a soft spot for banana bread and fresh-baked goods generally)
My new socks
The million-dollar bacon at First Watch

It also includes people who continue to follow and support me. Things get added sort of randomly. Today it might be a new T-shirt that I like or a matcha drink. I've been convinced that anything with matcha or dark chocolate in it is good for me.

This will work for anyone. Write down a list of things that you're grateful for as a note on your phone. And then check it out regularly and add something. It will improve your frame of mind every time, guaranteed.

SERIOUSLY: STOP WHAT YOU ARE DOING AND MAKE AT LEAST ONE OF THESE LISTS. ONE FOR YOUR GOALS, ANOTHER WITH THINGS YOU ARE GRATEFUL FOR. This could be the most valuable chapter in this book.

Goals and Gratitude. Those are the two lists that make every day a little bit better and make the world go around. And take yourself seriously enough to check off a goal or three.

So I know what you're thinking: *Did he actu-*

ally go skydiving? Yes, I did, with some friends in upstate New York when I turned thirty. But you know what's even better? Hang gliding. Wasn't even on my list. You can go off-book whenever you want.

Chapter 14
Linsanity

In 2012, a guy named Jeremy Lin burst onto the scene.

Jeremy Lin hit my radar while he was a point guard on the basketball team at Harvard, my parents' dream school. He had some big games against other Division 1 teams. I thought to myself, *This could be the best Asian American hooper in a generation.* I brought Evelyn to see him play a college game in New York City; we met him afterward and had him sign a T-shirt.

I figured Jeremy would play overseas. This became all the more likely when he went undrafted at the end of his college career. Then he got signed by the Golden State Warriors to a development contract, but it seemed more like a feel-good story than a serious investment.

Jeremy was cut by the Warriors and then signed with the Knicks. My dream for most of my life was to be *backup* point guard for the Knicks.

(Even in my dreams I couldn't imagine being the starting point guard.)

Jeremy was literally living my dream. And then *Linsanity* happened.

The Knicks won a game with Jeremy coming off the bench and scoring twenty-five points. Then Jeremy was starting and scored twenty-eight. He dropped thirty-eight points against Kobe Bryant and the Los Angeles Lakers in a nationally televised game. He hit the game-winner in Toronto. The whole thing was like a fever dream come true. Evelyn became a fan for the first time, saying, "I didn't know this sport could be so much fun!" We watched every game as the Knicks won eight in a row.

Jeremy got injured shortly thereafter and missed the playoffs. But I figured we had many years to root for him. The Knicks didn't lose their own free agents over money. Jeremy had lit up Madison Square Garden and all of New York City. He was insanely marketable and only twenty-four years old. This was a team that had been looking for an answer at point guard for as long as I could remember. There was no way we would let a player we discovered walk.

I was wrong.

The Knicks didn't match a contract offer from the Houston Rockets. Knicks superstar Carmelo Anthony called the contract "ridiculous." Jeremy Lin, the darling of New York City, was being jettisoned against his will. It felt like getting punched in the gut.

The Knicks were known for overpaying their players. This was the same team that had given players like Jerome James, Eddy Curry, and Jared Jeffries terrible massive contracts as free agents. And even if you wanted to trade Jeremy later, he'd be an asset given his marketability.

Nope. He was gone.

As you can imagine, I was pissed off. My vision of rooting for the scrappy Asian American point guard on my hometown team was replaced with a sense of betrayal. I decided I could no longer support the Knicks and I broke up with them. I tossed out my Knicks cap and paraphernalia. Some of my friends tried to talk me out of it. "I'm pissed too, man, but the team is still good." I just couldn't do it anymore. I had rooted for this team even through the lousy Isiah Thomas era, through years of mismanagement. But this was a bridge too far. Fuck these guys and fuck the team owner, James Dolan.

I became something of a basketball vagabond. I rooted for Jeremy as he went to the Rockets, then the Lakers, the Charlotte Hornets, and finally the Brooklyn Nets, whom I adopted as my new team. When Jeremy arrived in Brooklyn, I took my family to go see him. Barclays Center didn't feel as iconic as the Garden, but at least the tickets were more affordable.

A few years later, in 2019, I was running for president. I was asked about sports teams, the Knicks in particular. They were in the midst of a long dry spell. I said, "Banning Charles Oakley wasn't right. Nor is banning fans from games for voicing their opinions. James Dolan should sell the team. That would show that he really wants to do the right thing by New York." It was the kind of comment you would see in online forums and hear on the streets all the time.

To my shock, the Garden put out a press release: *Andrew Yang should keep his mouth shut.* It went on to talk trash about me and my campaign. How thin-skinned would you have to be?

A couple years later, I ran afoul of the Garden again when I commented that they didn't pay property taxes, and they should. Dolan literally threatened to move the arena. Like that would ever happen. Where would he move it to, New Jersey?

I'm glad I stopped giving James Dolan my time and money. I wish the Knicks well because they're good for New York and so many of my friends cheer for them. Jalen Brunson and Josh Hart seem like great guys. But now I feel the same way about them as I would an ex-girlfriend: I wish them well but I'm happy to have moved on. I thought that the firing of Coach Tom Thibodeau after the 2025 playoff run was classic Dolan— that's not a compliment.

People matter more than jerseys.

Also, Jeremy Lin is a really nice guy. Thanks

for the memories, Jeremy! You lived my dream and the dreams of a lot of other people.

NBA champ!

Part III

JUST DO EVERYTHING RIGHT

Chapter 15
Choosing to Run

My career is going pretty well. How can I make everyone think that I'm crazy?

I hear nice things about Iowa. How about I spend a few months there in the winter?

How can I avoid my wife and kids for the better part of two years?

The reason you're reading this book is most likely because I ran for president. Why did I do it? The official reason—I'm an awesome human being. The unofficial reason is more complicated. I knew that AI was coming and would chew up a ton of jobs. Heck, this book could all be AI-generated and you might not know. I had spent six years marching around the country saying, "Let's revitalize the country through entrepreneurship." I concluded in 2017 that AI was going to do a number on the average American's job. So what does one do at that point?

I thought there was a 15 percent chance I could speed up the end of poverty if we got forty thousand

Iowans on board. That seemed like a fine investment of a few years of my time. Thanks for getting behind me if you did! If you didn't, congratulations—people are still poor because of you.

If you're sincere, you try to alert the country.

Plus, I got a sinking feeling in my stomach watching Trump win. I don't hate him or Trumpers like a lot of people do. But I felt his election was bad news for the country. You know in *Dune* how "fear is the mind-killer"? That's how I feel about Donald Trump: he's the mind-killer.

A very big influence for me was Andy Stern's book *Raising the Floor*. Toward the end of the book, Stern states his belief that "someone should run as a presidential candidate on this issue," referring to UBI. I read it and said to myself, *Yeah, that's a good idea, someone should totally do that.*

But running for president was, in retrospect, a rash idea. My mom tried to talk me out of it, and she's generally pretty optimistic. So why did I do it?

One thing I had going for me is something called "irrational self-confidence." I met three of the last four presidents while I was running Venture for America: Bill Clinton, George W. Bush, and Barack Obama. You know what I didn't think? *Wow, these guys are amazing. I could never do what they do. So impressive. So profound.*

Instead it was more like, *Meh. Just a dude.*

Tall, yes. Superhuman, no.

This was even more true when I met governors, senators, congresspeople, mayors, etc. Most of the time they were fine, likable people and pretty good in a room. But it wasn't like, *These politicians are phenomenal!* What I felt most often wasn't awe or admiration, but more like sympathy because their jobs seemed so repetitive and unappealing.

I remember feeling this again during the 2016 Republican primary. It was Jeb Bush, Marco Rubio, Ben Carson, Rick Perry, Ted Cruz, Carly Fiorina, and the eventual winner, Donald Trump. I watched it on TV thinking, *These people are pretty average.* Trump was the most talented performer among them, in that he could hold your attention and make an argument, even if it was off base or overly simplistic.

Okay, so I kind of thought I could run and do some good and not be out of my depth. Still, why spend months trying to do the nearly impossible? A major reason was my experience becoming a dad.

Chapter 16
Falling Down the Food Chain

I became a father on October 31, 2012. Hurricane Sandy blew through New York that night, causing power outages—it also caused a lot of women to go into labor because of the change in air pressure. Many kids were born that night.

I was excited to be a dad. It was one of my dreams come true. But I wasn't ready for what followed.

After we took our little bundle of joy home, there was a ton of stress in the apartment. Speaking for myself, you might be accustomed to mattering in your household. Pretty quickly, you don't. The family hierarchy before fatherhood was:

1. You and your partner, maybe about equally
2. The dog
3. Friends and others

You're living the life of a couple with an active social world. You might get dinner with another couple to catch up. And as a couple with a dog, that dog is like your child—a fuzzy, wordless, adorable little child who needs to be walked a few times a day. Life is pretty good.

That arrangement became this:

1. The baby
2. The baby
3. The baby
4. The baby
5. The baby
6. The baby
7. The baby
8. The baby
9. The baby
10. The baby
11. Mommy
12. Anyone who helps Mommy

    .

    .

    .

    .

    .

18. You
19. The dog
20. We have friends?

I was demoted approximately seventeen rungs. It did not help that every morning when our son Christopher woke up, he would look around the room and his face would slowly scrunch into a scowl. Then he would start to cry at the top of his lungs, as if to say, *Why am I still here??? Waaaaaaah!* He was a difficult baby.

I would find myself in the doghouse, literally and figuratively. Each night, I would take our dog Grizzly for a walk and sit with him on a bench. He's a Havanese so he looks very wise with his fur covering his chin, like the beard of a kind old man. We would look at one another and I would say, "Well, at least we have each other."

I now regard the above as a natural course of things and why we're all alive. I try to tell expecting dads, "Biology is the most powerful force in the world." Also, "Whatever you experience, it's totally normal." Driving around aimlessly in the middle of the night to keep your child from waking? Totally normal. Putting your hand out to catch your child's dump at a party because you are at a total loss as to what else to do and you're trying to keep him from making a mess? Sure, why not.

Why would my struggles as a first-time parent lead me to run for president? I was a bit cocky going into it. I was like, *People have been producing kids since the dawn of time, how hard could it be?* There were two of us. I also thought that we had lots of advantages, including above-average levels of resources.

So dumb. You know what the best resource

is when you have a child? Family members who want to spend time with your kid who aren't getting paid to do so.

A friend of mine put it to me in a way I remember: "It's the first time in your life you can't just work your way out of it." It's a stretching of the soul. It nearly broke me.

But what really hit me was that if it was this hard for me and Evelyn, how hard would it be for parents and families who didn't have as much going for them? How were kids going to grow up out there?

Chapter 17

The Wilderness

When I told friends I was running for president, the most common response was something like, "Of what, your co-op board?" People were not encouraging. Maybe they had talked to my mom.

Perhaps I wasn't as cool as I'd thought?

One friend said something I appreciated a great deal: "That seems crazy. But I said you were crazy before and you proved me wrong. I told myself after that, *Okay, whatever Andrew tells you he's doing, just support him.* So this time, I'm in."

I officially declared my presidential run in February 2018 with an article in the *New York Times* called "His 2020 Campaign Message: The Robots Are Coming."

It did not take the world by storm.

I make the same mistake over and over again: I think the next thing is going to be like the last thing. I thought running for president was going to be something like starting a wholesome entrepreneurship nonprofit: you talk to people, make your case, present a vision, and get people on board.

But running for president was much more about me and who I was. I initially wanted to call the campaign "UBI2020," for Universal Basic Income. But someone said, "That sounds like a urinary tract infection." "Yang2020" was much better, though that required me to be the front man and own it.

Try something for me: find a roommate or friend or your partner, take them by the shoulders and say to them, "I'm running for president of the United States of America." It feels ridiculous, right? Like you immediately want to follow it up with, "I'm just kidding! This book asked me to say it to you, it's not real." It felt that way for me too for quite a while. And the reactions didn't help.

It took me about a year to be able to say it to a stranger with a straight face, without any hint of irony or self-deprecation or doubt. For the most part it was incredibly awkward. I would go to my kids' school events and avoid questions about what I did for a living, because saying "I'm a presidential candidate" made me seem like an absolute lunatic. Imagine some dad at the potluck telling you that? Plus, if you do decide to tell them, it takes fifteen minutes to explain, and at the end they never say, "Let me help! Where do I donate or volunteer?"

Instead, I'd get a confused, "Interesting . . .

good luck with that." Who wants to have that conversation over and over again?

Running for president without the virtues of fame, title, fortune, crowd support, social media following, etc., was a real education in humility. We had events where no one showed up. Who wants to hear from the random guy with delusions of grandeur?

Not many people, it turns out.

So how did we get through those early weeks? You take it day by day. But we had some things going for us. First, we had a fun, scrappy young team of true believers. Who would sign up for the Yang campaign as a wise career choice? Everyone on staff was driven by the truth of the message. Thanks to Zach Graumann in particular.

Second, we had a sense of humor about our situation. We didn't take ourselves that seriously.

Third, we seized on anything positive and made a big deal out of it. Anytime someone donated to our campaign, even if it was five dollars, we would ring a bell in our little office. I would then email or call that person to thank them. For a long time, I was thanking friends of mine, who totally deserved it! But sometimes I'd be thanking a stranger, and they'd seem surprised and thrilled to hear from me. Pretty soon the newcomers outnumbered the people I knew.

Zach told me to get good at social media, because it was free. I put energy into that. This would eventually help us grow. We said yes to any interview or event, no matter how small or niche-y. "Ask Me Anything" on Reddit? Sure! Interview with a tech website? Definitely. And then we thanked them and amplified it even if they were slightly snarky in the coverage.

One question I would get a lot in those early interviews: "Are you serious? Do you think you can win?" It's a bit of a trick question, because if you say yes, you're crazy. But if you say no, you're a joke. So you have to come up with a third answer, something like: "This is a campaign of ideas." Or, "There are multiple versions of victory."

A few words I would use to sum up running for president in those early days are *camera angles*, *rental cars*, and *rest stops*. Let's say we had a campaign event in South Carolina and ten people showed up. If you pile those ten people into the same picture, plus yourself, plus maybe a staffer or two, you could make it look like an okay event, if . . . you get the right camera angle. With the wrong camera angle, it appears desolate and empty. So a lot of energy was spent arranging people and trying to get the right angle. A dud becomes a quality pic with the right caption: *Talking to voters in Columbia, South Carolina—they're excited about the campaign!*

I spent a ton of time in rental cars. In Iowa and New Hampshire, rentals are the only way to get around. At one point, my cameraperson was doubling as my driver. It was late at night in Iowa heading to our hotel, and he almost hit a divider. He was not inspiring confidence, despite being stone-cold sober. Trying not to be obnoxious, I asked, "Hey, out of curiosity, have you ever been in any car accidents?"

"Yeah, four, but none of them were my fault."

I paused. "Great. Can you stop at this next gas station? I could use a bathroom break." Then, after I came out, I said, "Hey, I feel like driving. Just to relax. Can I take it from here?" There was no way I was going to wake up in a ditch because my cameraperson couldn't drive.

When you're crisscrossing these states so much, the rest stops become havens. A lot of the time, because of your schedule, you're eating rest stop food as a meal, which isn't great. I got super excited to head into a rest stop to pick up a meal of mixed nuts, sunflower seeds, a KIND bar, popcorn, and some iced tea. My favorite rest stop chain name in Iowa was Kum & Go, which had its name changed in 2023. I wonder why? It pains me that I will never go into a Kum & Go again.

People ask me how I had the perseverance to run. Sometimes I ask entrepreneurs, "If you were to decide to start a business, how much time have you just signed up for?" They think for a minute. Typical responses include:

"Five years."

"Eight years?"

"I don't know. Because you can't know."

"That's right!" I reply. "This means running for office is easier than starting a business." By deciding to run for president, I knew I was signing up for three years of campaigning. More likely it was going to be two and a half years since I probably wouldn't get past the primaries. "If I told you that you'd have to knock yourself out and do everything right for two and a half years, could you do it?" This question made it seem more doable.

The moment I told my friends I was running and took a dollar from them, I signed up to do my utmost through the finish line. In the tough early days, I tried to make each day a little better than the one before. I believed in the case I was making because I knew it had the virtue of being true—AI was coming. I had to let people know. I was like Jon Snow in *Game of Thrones,* except I knew who my parents were.

Chapter 18

My Inner Rock

Fifteen months later, I would be standing in front of thousands of people chanting my name. We had a rally in Los Angeles in 2019 that drew seven thousand people.

How did we get from zero people showing up to thousands?

If you're reading this, you probably know the

answer since you were part of it. Everyday Americans started to get behind the campaign and told their friends about it. They donated one dollar and told family members to do the same so that I'd make a debate stage. *Google Andrew Yang* and *#YangGang* became things. So did the *MATH* cap.

The main lesson I took was this—the more human I got, the better we did. When I started, my stump speech was a pretty dry, lucid talk on AI, automation, Universal Basic Income, the labor force, and the impact of the fourth industrial revolution. It was interesting to a select group of people, but it didn't spread like wildfire.

Every once in a while, though, I'd show some emotion. And then people would light up. Shed a tear over the future of the country? Get hardcore volunteers in New Hampshire. Get pissed off about our soulless bureaucracy in DC? Pick up superfans who follow the campaign everywhere. Become indignant over widespread poverty? Gain some charged-up ministers and creatives.

It was in some ways the opposite of being corporate, because being a business guy generally required being rational and unemotional in most every circumstance. You don't want Businessperson getting upset or emotional. You want him or her to be upbeat and numbers-driven, measured and cool. Businessperson is competent and judicious. If he or she shows emotion, it should be in a narrow band. A corporate leader is allowed an outburst only infrequently, and even then it's probably not a good thing.

For politics it was kind of the opposite—people craved emotion. It was less about *what* and more about *why?* When people thought I was fired up or passionate or sad, it gave them license to care. I felt like my campaigning day and night for months should have been enough, but that didn't necessarily translate the way an emotional moment would. The deeper I dug, the more it clicked for people that I was doing it all for them and their families.

It extended into frivolities too. Do the Cupid Shuffle in South Carolina? Chance the Rapper nods approvingly and CNN runs the clip. Kick a bottle cap off a soda bottle? Get millions of views and new fans. Basically, the more I seemed like a real person, the more excited people got. Zach would say to me, "People love surprises. No one expects the Asian tech guy to get pissed off or emotional. It gives you a new dimension."

Writing down the ideas of the campaign in *The War on Normal People* helped too. 175,000 people bought copies of that book and a lot of them joined the YangGang. Dave Chappelle told me later that someone just left him a copy of my book and he read it before reaching out to the campaign.

It all took me by surprise. I vividly remember in early 2019 being stuck in traffic on the way to a rally in San Francisco. I said to Zach, "What's with all of this traffic?" Then I saw a *Yang* sign in one of the cars blocking our way and exclaimed, "Holy shit, this is *our* traffic!!!" A couple thousand people showed up to that rally and that kind of turnout became the norm from then on.

Rallies always felt special. Imagine having thousands of people come together for you, chanting your name. The energy was palpable. I felt supercharged every time and tried to give that energy back to the attendees in any way I could. If you attended a rally, thank you!

How best to pump up a crowd? I channeled some of my favorite pro wrestlers: two of my biggest influences were the Rock and Diamond Dallas Page. I had catchphrases, like "Powerpoint," "Hello YangGang—you don't look like the Internet to me!" and "The opposite of Donald Trump is an Asian man who likes MATH!" I made my hand into a claw that represented Amazon sucking money out of communities. At that event in LA when people started chanting "*Yang beats Trump,*" I responded, "That's right, Yang *does* beat Trump! It's like a game of rock-paper-scissors. And if Donald Trump is the scissors, then I'm the fucking rock!"

You inhabit the message and see what comes out. It turns out that my communication style leant itself to memes.

The Rock said that his wrestling persona was like his personality turned up to eleven; it's him, but an amplified version. That's what it felt like. It was me, but a bigger, most boisterous version. Rallies became a lot of fun. The energy was so high that at one event I crowd-surfed, which made the news. I hadn't crowd-surfed since my teenage years at Lollapalooza.

I did numerous podcast interviews during this time. The Joe Rogan podcast was a huge catalyst for the campaign. There was pretty much a *before Rogan* and *after Rogan* effect. Other major shows like *Real Time with Bill Maher* and *The View* moved the needle too. My social media presence grew as we broadcast whatever we were doing on any given day.

What was it like being on the inside of the vortex? The oddest thing was being recognized on the street. The first time it happened, I thought it was a fluke. Evelyn started saying, "I can't take you anywhere," because people would stop us and want to talk and take pictures. Folks were always very lovely and excited.

Out on the trail, I met three people who had tattoos of me or the campaign's logo on their body. Two of them seemed healthy and well-balanced. The third . . . not so much.

It felt a little bit like a double life. There was my campaign life, complete with team, entourage, rental vehicles, and uniform that included a *MATH* pin and flag scarf. Then there was my home life, when I would act like a homebody for thirty-six hours and wear jeans and a hoodie and play with my kids.

Aside from the rallies, some of the most memorable nights were the presidential debates. I had no idea what I was in for. I'd find out the hard way.

Chapter 19

Competitive Theater

In the middle of 2019, the presidential debates began. They started out with twenty candidates spread out over two nights. The qualifications were 65,000 donors and at least 1 percent polling. People were pumped for me to get on the debate stage, which I appreciated.

I made seven debates and they were very weird experiences. What were they like in real life? I had a very bad first debate. I didn't understand the assignment. It wasn't a debate; it was a competitive theater performance. First, you arrive at least ninety minutes beforehand with your team. You're stuck in a green room and it's kind of awkward, in part because there is typically another candidate in the room next to you and their staff is walking around. It's not generally the type of environment where people feel like they can talk freely. So you are pretty quiet, reviewing your notes and trying to get in the right frame of mind while your staff tries not to act nervous. You record a couple videos saying, "Tune in tonight and thank you for getting me here!"

The network takes you into a makeup room where their team goes crazy with makeup for TV debates. I felt like the actor who played Data in *Star Trek*—the makeup was so heavy. I even mentioned it in one debate—"We're all up here with makeup on our faces and our rehearsed attack lines"—because it felt so staged.

You interact quite a lot with the other candidates because you're all lined up backstage. It was odd, people standing three feet behind another candidate, making small talk with someone else whom they're about to yell at in front of millions of people. I distinctly remember Bill de Blasio practicing his closing statement behind the curtain like it was a high school play. I shouldn't talk, as I sometimes jogged in place to get my energy up.

You can't see much of anything when you're up there because the stage lights are bright and in your eyes. You know when candidates look into the crowd and wave to people they recognize? I was just pretending.

There's a ton of memorization that goes into the debate. You have your opening, your closing, three to five messages that you're trying to get out there, and then various subject matter responses. It's like a weird oral examination in front of hundreds of audience members and then millions of people at home.

You know all of the scribbling and scrawling candidates are doing? Most of the time they're not taking notes on what other candidates are saying; they're jotting down reminders to themselves about what their closing statement is going to be. There's a lot of that going on. I had a cheat sheet I'd recreate at the podium for each debate with notes and instructions.

Because of all of the scripting, you tend to remember anything that is spontaneous or human. For me, that involved sticking up for Tom Steyer when people were giving him a hard time, or ad-libbing "Sorry I beat your guy" when asked what I would say to Putin.

Ahead of the third debate in Houston, I sat with my team. A consultant said, "This debate is going to be super boring because George Stephanopoulos is only going to ask policy questions. Americans will change the channel and no one is going to remember anything that's said."

"So, what's the plan then?" I asked.

"Well, we can just write this debate off as a dud. Or we can do something creative with your opening."

We considered for a bit. "What is this campaign about?" I asked. And then I answered my own question: "Giving people money. We should just give people money during my opener while viewers are still tuned in."

This divided the team.

"The press will hate it."

"It will make you seem unserious."

"You'll look like a game show host."

My idea was to give ten American families $1,000 a month for a year. "Guys," I said, "this is a high-variance campaign. We take swings. If we don't, we might as well just fold up shop now. Plus, at least this way we are guaranteed to help ten families."

We settled on it and I crafted a sixty-second message on why I was giving money away. Sure enough, it went over terribly with the media . . . and just great with the American people. Five million visitors went to the campaign website in the minutes after my statement. And donors to the campaign contributed another one million dollars in the next twenty-four hours—apparently, many people liked giving money to everyday Americans too.

The consultant was right as well—that's the only thing I remember from that debate. I should have gone even harder on giving money away, as meeting all of the families a few weeks later was one of my favorite days of the campaign. What can I say? Giving people money is fun.

I felt a lot more comfortable by the last debate—I had become a competitive theater performer. Would it be enough?

Chapter 20

The Last Stand

The campaign kept growing throughout the rest of 2019. In January of 2020, we went to Iowa to make our stand. We conducted a seventeen-day bus tour that crisscrossed the state. The best part was that at this stage it actually made sense to have a campaign bus, which is a whole lot more fun than the usual rental vehicle. My boys got to ride on the bus, played video games, and made some memories.

It was the "Month of Yang," as volunteers from all over the country arrived to try to get us our 40,000 Iowans. The "Sorority of Yang" hosted sixty volunteers. Everywhere I went in the state, there were people in *MATH* hats staffing campaign offices and knocking on doors. It felt like a little army was descending on the state to fight it out for the future of humanity. The winter conditions made it feel like a battlefront too, like the planet Hoth from *The Empire Strikes Back*. Thomas Wu, a volunteer from Oregon, dislocated a kneecap on ice while knocking on doors. He was literally in a wheelchair at an event. "That's a battlefield injury," I marveled.

I won the Iowa Youth Straw Poll, so if we'd just cut the voting age off at eighteen, I'd be president today. I was also #1 in "Candidate I'd want to have a beer with." If only that had been "Candidate I'm going to vote for." 61 percent of Iowans said they were open to supporting me, the same percentage that also supported giving everyone $1,000 a month.

Iowa has a loveliness to it in every season, including winter. The horizons stretch far into the distance and there's something quintessentially American about the sunsets. I enjoyed my time there and will always appreciate the people I met. The night of the caucuses, a very sweet old lady said to me, "Please run again." To which my internal response was, *Lady, I'm running right now!*

In the first round of voting, I got 8,914 votes, or about 24 percent of what I needed to flip the table. 5.1 percent of the Iowans who showed up that night caucused for me. Bernie Sanders would eventually go on to win the state with over 26 percent of the votes. I gave a glib address based on the fact that they couldn't yet report the votes with any confidence because of a tech snafu, and then hopped on a plane to New Hampshire.

There was only about a week until New Hampshire voted. We had six or seven events scheduled a day. There were press and crowds everywhere. The actor Paul Giamatti showed up to just check out the candidates—you really can do it in a couple days on a road trip. The roads in New Hampshire are a bit too narrow and windy for a bus in the winter if you're on a tight schedule, so it was back to rental cars.

I campaigned in Exeter, New Hampshire, and saw the parents of some of my high school classmates. I even bumped into an old teacher of mine. He better have voted for me.

I did a pretty good job of running through the tape. The results from Iowa, though, took a bit of wind out of our sails. The strongest candidates out of Iowa were Bernie and Pete Buttigieg, and that would happen again. Notably, Joe Biden would come in fourth with 15.8 percent of the vote.

During that week, my team came to me and told me that I should consider suspending the campaign if the results weren't good in New Hampshire. I resisted—as long as people still wanted me to keep going, I wanted to keep going. I thought I was the indefatigable Energizer Bunny candidate. I still felt that the hopes and dreams of so many people rested with me and the campaign. My team made the argument that I was also the MATH candidate—and the math said we couldn't win. Eventually, I agreed that if we didn't get any delegates in New Hampshire, we'd suspend the campaign.

Writing what was essentially a concession speech was heartwrenching. I didn't feel like anything was ending. After the New Hampshire primary didn't go my way, my speech included the words, "This is not an ending, this is just the beginning!" And I meant it. The next day, I went from New Hampshire to Nevada to thank supporters. Tears were shed.

Did it end the right way, and at the right time?

What I've come to realize is that there is no right way or time—and that campaigns always end suddenly and abruptly. One week you are riding high with crowds and energy, and the following week you are looking around at a room full of buttons, signs, and T-shirts, saying, "I wonder what we're going to do with all of this."

Chapter 21

The Three-Headed Monster

During the campaign, I made hundreds of political speeches and saw hundreds more. Most political communication, particularly on the Democratic side, is earnest and appeals to a sense of community. For example: "If you want to go fast, go alone, but if you want to go far, go together!" That's a Cory Booker message, but it would be appropriate from dozens of Democratic candidates. "Let's come together."

Bernie was more argumentative, saying things like: "The business model of Wall Street is fraud. The billionaires have rigged the economy while the working people of this country can't afford to pay an unexpected $400 bill!" His approach has a villain and a conflict, which makes it more exciting. Yet it's still very much a community-based message: *You, the listener, are part of the working people and we have to overcome the billionaires.*

Trump's approach is very different. It's much more highly individualistic:

"Only *I* can fix it."

"If you don't elect me, we won't have a country anymore."

"I'm the greatest dealmaker of all time, and we will have the biggest and best economy of all time."

Trump projects messianic vibes: *I'm great, I'm the best, I am one of one.* It's not politics-as-usual. You know what it reminds me of? Who else tells the world how great they are at every turn?

Pro wrestlers.

I watched a lot of pro wrestling as a kid, and the wrestlers were often very self-centered and braggadocious in their communication:

"I'm the best damn champion there ever was."

"Stone Cold 3:16 says I just whupped your ass!"

"I'm the Macho Man Randy Savage, the cream of the crop, and you're not! Ooooh yeah!"

"Finally . . . the Rock has come BACK to Pittsburgh!"

Pro wrestlers literally talk in the third person in order to emphasize how great they are. And they come complete with nicknames like "The Great One" or "The Showstopper" that they bestow upon themselves. Bret Hart went by "The Best There Is / The Best There Was / The Best There Ever Will Be"—and he was a good guy! Heck, Booker T became "King Bookah" and acted like a king.

This isn't any new or subtle connection. Our current president is a WWE Hall of Famer and

Wrestlemania bad guy, and his cabinet includes the co-owner of the WWE, Linda McMahon. Trump has been close friends with Vince McMahon for years. He has channeled pro wrestling–style self-promotion all the way to the top.

This self-hype does serve a purpose. It gives off a feeling of confidence and energy. It's also more individualistic, which appeals to certain people, particularly men. Note that pro wrestling shows are among the highest-rated shows week after week, much higher than, say, cable news programs.

Democrats have never understood this or had any response to it. And it's hard to imagine any of today's Democratic candidates embracing an "I'm the sole answer" persona. Can you imagine JB Pritzker giving this a try? *I've got the largest pythons in the world! Whatcha gonna do when Pritzkermania comes running wild on you!* For a Democrat, it would seem kind of bizarre.

So Trump has gotten access to a totally different energy and audience. But he doesn't stop there. He also exercises a communication form that may even exceed pro wrestling in its mass appeal. What am I talking about?

"Low-energy Jeb."

"Little Marco."

"Meatball Ron."

All of these nicknames made it into the zeitgeist.

So did "Crooked Hillary" and "Sleepy Joe."

Comedy. Donald Trump is a world-class insult comic.

You remember him in his last debate against Biden? "I really don't know what he said at the end of this and I don't think he knows what he said either." Trump constantly trash-talks his opponents at his rallies, running them down. It's consistently amusing to his people. Trump tries out each line in front of a live crowd and only when it clicks does he start using it a lot. He tests out material and then runs with it. It's exactly what a comedian would do.

When is the last time you saw a Democrat be funny? It's all earnestness and lists of issues, even while most of the issues have been getting worse in real life for years. When they try to do something humorous, it mostly makes you cringe. Their funniest guy, Al Franken, got drummed out of the party for some ill-advised photographs.

Democrats have become the de facto defenders of institutions that most Americans have turned on. How are you feeling about government, democracy, the economy, or the media nowadays? They are defending a shrinking island in a time of surging bullshit. Trust you? *Nah. I'd trust you more if you seemed like you were super into yourself or funny, because then maybe I'd believe you were a normal person. Otherwise it looks like you're playacting at being a do-gooder who is probably full of shit.*

All the hours I spent watching pro wrestling

when I was a kid were VERY handy when I ran for president.

The problem for the Democrats is that they *practice* politics. Fewer and fewer Americans respond to that language or consume news media, particularly men without college degrees. They are much more likely to watch a sporting event, pro wrestling show, or comedy podcast. Meanwhile, Democrats devote a great deal of time talking to college grads when about two-thirds of Americans don't have a college degree.

When a Democrat asked me how to fix the party, I responded, "Watch UFC and WWE programming for three months."

Pro wrestling and comedy overlap in that they have anti-institutional, countercultural energy. Trump has *combined* these three previously separate modes of communication: politics, pro wrestling, and comedy. They simply reach more people across more platforms.

What are the takeaways from this?

When J.D. Vance or Eric Trump Jr. or Josh Hawley or whoever tries to channel Trump, it doesn't work because they look like they are . . . a politician trying to impersonate Trump. They're acting, badly. They don't have either the pro wrestling persona or the comedic energy to pull it off. Trump's movement and appeal will not transfer to others within the Republican Party.

The efforts to identify a "liberal Joe Rogan" are

a waste of time. Joe Rogan is naturally a highly individualistic countercultural voice. Note that Rogan is a stand-up comic and a high-level mixed martial arts expert and commentator himself. The only time I considered joining the Trump team was when Trump started walking into UFC events with cabinet members. I'd watch it on TV and think, *That's dope! Maybe I should give them a call.* Of course I wouldn't actually do that, but I was impressed.

If a high-level pro wrestler or comedian were to run for office, they would probably do surprisingly well. The Rock or John Cena would kill on the trail. So would Dave Chappelle, Jon Stewart, or Chris Rock. Volodymyr Zelensky started out as a comedian in Ukraine before becoming president.

When you ask voters what they want in a candidate nowadays, a word that comes up a lot is *authenticity.* Wrestlers and comedians seem authentic because they're each channeling a language that speaks to basic human impulses. Wrestlers are self-promoting warrior-performers. Comedians are truthtellers. One reason my campaign caught on is that I seemed like an actual person; voters sensed that the machine would never send out an anonymous Asian guy trying to give everyone free money. I tried to have fun as a survival tactic. And I might not be a pro wrestler, but I did start a gang, which is a very pro wrestler thing to do.

Chapter 22

Inspired by the *Onion*

Coming back to "normal" life after the campaign was jarring. I felt like I had been holding a live wire and then let go of it. I took a hike and looked up into the sky for a day or two.

But the energy around me was still super high. Everyone wanted to know what I was doing next. I got calls for endorsements from Bernie, Biden, Bloomberg—all of the B's. More directly, I still had a team around me that was trying to figure out our next moves.

My main inspiration was where we all go for purpose: the *Onion*, the satirical news and media company. Back in 2010, I read an *Onion* article that made me laugh out loud: "American People Hire High-Powered Lobbyist to Push Interests in Congress." The article has a picture of a slightly tool-y-looking guy in a suit named Jack Weldon saying, "Now they'll take us seriously!"

The imaginary lobbyist Weldon goes on to say, "To be honest, the American people have always been perceived as a little naive when it comes to their representative government. But having me on their side sends a clear message that they're finally serious and want to play ball."

I found this to be hysterical and brilliant—who does represent the American people on Capitol Hill? Why don't ordinary people hire a lobbyist?

Ten years later, after I came off the presidential trail, I found myself living a version of this article; I started a nonprofit, Humanity Forward, that would lobby for an end to poverty. We started off intending to pilot cash-relief programs in various communities. Then COVID hit.

The world shut down. No one knew how people would get by. So we pivoted to simply giving money away. First, we decided to give $1,000 to 1,000 families in the Bronx. Where did we get this money? A bunch of people donated to Humanity Forward when we launched it, including Twitter cofounder Jack Dorsey, who put in $10 million. If you donated, thank you! We put the money to good use, as you'll see. We were literally Robin Hood during the pandemic. What's funny is that giving away money is actually easier said than done.

We called Citibank and JPMorgan Chase and said, "Hey, can you identify 1,000 families in the Bronx with low cash balances? We'd like to give them money."

What do you think they both said? "No. There

are rules against that." Rules against someone giving their customers money! I doubt the customers would have complained.

So we got creative. We found another nonprofit, Neighborhood Trust, that provides financial services to the working poor. They were happy to distribute the money to 1,000 families and even threw in a financial counseling session.

Then, as the economy started to shut down, we gave another 20,000 people micro-grants of between $250 and $500. This time, we did it over Venmo and PayPal. Sometimes we sent as little as $20 just to let someone know that we did indeed see them. In total, we sent out about $5 million this way in 2020.

We did this in part to try to push Congress to issue cash relief during COVID. Every day I would Zoom with a different member of Congress to talk about how popular and necessary stimulus checks were. I did this with over sixty congresspeople. It worked! Stimulus checks of $600 went out in January 2021, followed by an additional $1,400 later that spring. I got hundreds, maybe thousands of messages of appreciation as those checks started arriving in people's accounts.

Humanity Forward went on to become a full-fledged advocacy organization in Washington, DC, lobbying for the people. The executive director is Liam deClive-Lowe, a political prodigy who worked on my presidential campaign. Even now, Liam and his colleagues wear suits every day, meet members of Congress, share survey data, connect with chiefs of staff, and so much more. Their message is something like: "Hey, we asked, and it turns out your constituents don't like poor kids. Not that they don't like the kids themselves. They don't like that so many are poor. So . . . if you were to make some of them a little less poor, your voters would like you a little better."

The response: "Wait, who do you represent? And how did you get in this office?"

Kidding! Their real pitch is more like, "Hey, there are lots of bipartisan or nonpartisan things worth doing with your time in Congress that would assist many people, and we'd like to help you make them happen. We're sure that some of the things you want to achieve aren't super partisan, so what can we do from outside Congress to make taking on those projects easier? How can we take the risk out of working with folks you might not have worked with before?"

Does this work? Over the years, I have picked up a few things by talking to lobbyists, legislators, and their teams. First, public-pressure tactics don't work. Yelling at an officeholder to support an agenda often makes it impossible for them to actually do it. *If you attack us and we cave and do it, it makes us appear weak. So yelling at us will actually decrease the chances of it happening.* It's a little bit like communicating with your partner: yelling seldom makes the situation better and generally makes it worse. You've got to convey the message in the right way, generally privately.

Second, DC is a town that runs on gossip and appearance. So if you want to build relationships with chiefs of staff and policy teams in congresspeople's offices, you have to be able to keep a secret and occasionally pass along information that can be helpful. Nobody likes a blabbermouth.

Third, everyone has a goal. For a member of Congress, it's to achieve the mission they were sent to Washington to do; sometimes that's harder than it might seem. For a staffer, it's to be connected with opportunities and to look good for their boss. If you help someone achieve a goal, you can make progress.

It turns out that lobbying works. A $2 million investment in lobbying in 2020 helped contribute to over $200 billion in cash-relief payments in both the stimulus checks and the enhanced, monthly child tax credit in 2021. It was my highest professional achievement, until Congress let the tax credit's temporary boost expire in 2022.

Ah, politics. But the organization Humanity Forward, based on the *Onion* article, is still in Washington, DC, doing its thing every day. It's something I'm immensely proud of, and you should be proud too if you supported my campaign. Thank you, *Onion*, for the inspiration! Keep up the great work.

Chapter 23

COVID Confessions

I have a confession—I kind of enjoyed COVID times. That's why I released the virus in the first place. Kidding! But I had been on the road so much that being stuck at home with my family was something of a relief.

I Zoomed for hours a day, of course. I joked that Zoom runs on human souls. I shouldn't say that because I know the person who founded Zoom, and he's a great guy. He doesn't seem to have any more soul energy than a normal person.

I wound up endorsing Joe Biden after the nomination was already in hand and became a surrogate for the campaign. Joe said to me multiple times on the trail, "If I win, get ready because you're coming to DC with me." I believe he was sincere, but I also don't think he was the one running the show. I didn't really hear from him or his team after the jobs started getting filled. I would later seek revenge.

I'm half glad he didn't offer me a job, as I was

on the record that I would have taken a role if I was offered something that would help the American people. My quote to CNN was, "Sure, I'd take a meaningful job if offered, because I'm not an asshole."

Four years later, I would get approached through the grapevine about whether I would consider joining the second Biden administration. I was like, "There's going to be a *second* Biden administration?!?"

I started going on TV as a commentator during COVID, which was a head trip. I was accustomed to hating those appearances. My quote to Zach was, "If after all of this I wind up a talking head, come shoot me in the face."

Since we were in the middle of a global pandemic, CNN started sending a mobile studio to my house for me to do segments. I would put on a shirt and jacket, but since no one could see my bottom half, I wore shorts and sandals. It was phenomenal just walking to my driveway, getting into a van, doing a TV hit, and then coming back inside and taking off my shirt and jacket and kicking back, all within half an hour. Did I mention that I enjoyed this time period?

After the election, I went down to Atlanta to campaign for a couple of Senate races. I campaigned with Martin Luther King III, who was very popular in town. Everyone greeted him like family. I got to visit Martin Luther King Jr.'s family home with his son, which was an experience that I'll never forget, as well as the King Center. There was a large inscription describing MLK's dedication to overcoming three societal evils: poverty, racism, and war.

Wow, those three really do sum it up, I thought. End poverty, overcome racism, and avoid war, and you really are in a much better place.

The Dems won both Senate races. While I was in Georgia, I started taking calls about running for mayor of New York. At first I was hesitant. But I was eventually convinced to run. We all know how that turned out.

Part IV

MODERN ADVENTURES

(Okay, so most of this book so far has been either my background or backstage during periods that you kind of know about or remember. The next stuff, you might not know about or don't remember. Let the mystery be revealed!)

Chapter 24
Leaving the Party

When my book *Forward: Notes on the Future of Our Democracy* came out at the end of 2021, I left the Democratic Party. I put out a little social media video and a brief blog post saying I was now an Independent.

People lost their minds. It made national head-lines. Millions of people googled me. Millions read the blog post—I wished I had been more lengthy and prosaic in my explanation. I got accused of being a wannabe Fox anchor, a grifter, a loser, a whiner, out to profit by selling books, and on and on. It was very odd.

The bookselling thing was particularly weird. You don't actually make money on books most of the time, and Democrats are big book buyers. Trying to become a gazillionaire as an author by leaving the Dems would be insane. How much am I getting paid to write *this* book? I don't even know, but let's just say it's not paying for anyone's college tuition. Maybe enough to buy some textbooks? Tell you what, I hereby pledge to donate all proceeds from this book to an antipoverty or democracy reform organization. Now you can tell others about it and know that the money is going someplace good! This pledge isn't hard to make because, again, there's isn't that much money at stake, unless this book becomes a mega-hit, at which point I retract this pledge and will instead bathe in the money.

I had been a CNN contributor up through this time. I was getting paid something pretty significant—about $125,000 a year—to be exclusive to them. Evelyn thought it was the best job I'd ever had. "You simply talk for a few minutes and they pay you? Keep that job!!" It was a lot easier going on air when they just ask you your opinion on something, rather than speaking as a candidate. They offered me a contract to return at the end of my mayoral run.

Then the news came out that I was no longer a Democrat. My agent called me during this time and said, "Hey, CNN is rescinding its offer to you. Apparently, they don't want to be seen as supporting a third party."

I responded, "Wouldn't that make me *more* valuable to them, not less, in that I'd be an objective voice that isn't tied up in one party or the other?"

"They don't think so."

"Huh. Okay." It felt like rejection from a company that I thought really liked me.

So there was a lot of blowback when I left the Democratic Party. I was more mystified by it than anything else. This was just me doing what I thought was the right thing.

On the TV front, I thought, *Okay, I guess this means I can go on any network. That's cool.* Fox started asking me to come on frequently.

I did that a couple times but became uncomfortable when a lot of it was, "Boy, those Democrats sure suck, don't they? Tell us more, Yang, you're a former Democrat: why'd you leave those idiots?" I left the Democratic Party because I had become convinced that their approach wasn't going to work, but it wasn't like I thought Fox and the Republicans were the answer.

It was a lesson: In order to feed the narrative machine, it paid to be on one side or the other. That's where the energy was. That's where the money was. I, of course, wasn't really motivated by that. But it definitely made me understand what other people go through when they're trying to do something a little bit different outside the machine.

During this time, my phone rang one afternoon. It was Dave Chappelle. We are friends but he doesn't often just ring me out of the blue. "Hey, man, I just called to say it's inspiring to see someone do something that is actually courageous. I never see that happen. But seeing you do it makes me feel like there's still some character left in the world. So thank you." I guess he'd heard that I'd left the party and was taking shit for it.

"Thanks, Dave, that means a lot." And it did. Take it from a guy who walked away from $50 million to do a comedy show with his name on it.

Dave's call was a pick-me-up. But my response to the blowback I was getting was also kind of contrarian and stubborn—it made me feel like I was on the right track. And I was confident I'd find others like me who didn't think the current path was going to work.

Chapter 25
The Secret of Writing

The secret of writing is to write. Just get stuff down. You can always edit it and make it better later. You don't even have to show anyone. Like a nerdy Nike slogan: Just Write It.

Chapter 26

My Poems

One fall evening in New York, Evelyn and I were hosted for dinner by a movie director in her brownstone on the Upper East Side. It was a lovely meal. Afterward, we went to our host's living room where she had a small surprise.

"Here, Andrew, I'd like to have you sign these for me." She brought out copies of my books. I was, of course, immensely flattered. Ordinarily, in this circumstance I might have brought a book with me, but she had already bought one of each: *Smart People Should Build Things, The War on Normal People,* and *Forward.*

Also a book of poetry by Andrew Yang called *Dear Me. My personal journey from darkness. For when you feel you've lost it all.*

Wait, what?

I looked at the small book of poems in her hand. It was featureless black. Just *Dear Me.* and the subtitles on the front and nothing identifiable on the back. No author photo, nothing.

"I didn't write this," I explained as I opened the book.

"No? Well that explains quite a bit," she said cryptically.

Evelyn found this hysterical. "Let me see that!" she chirped, and started leafing through it. "Oh my God, these are hilarious!"

Hilarity is not what the author intended. The poems are about his internal suffering, the journey he went through. I was ticked off and mortified.

When Evelyn and I got home, she searched for it on Amazon. There it was. There is no description. If someone just searches *Books by Andrew Yang*, multiple poetry volumes come up.

People were buying these books imagining that I was baring my soul! I considered tweeting something like, *FYI, there are some books of poetry out there by someone named Andrew Yang—they are NOT mine*, but this would likely have the effect of making more people aware of them. (This, by the way, is a constant concern, where if you react to something you elevate the attention paid to it.)

There was part of me that was irritated. Was someone actively impersonating me to sell books? Another part of me was slightly saddened for the author, if he was indeed named Andrew Yang and these were actually his poems. Keep in mind that I've met about half a dozen Andrew Yangs in my travels. While I was running for president, occasionally someone would come up to me and say, "Hey, I'm Andrew Yang too!" and show me their ID to prove it.

"Awesome!" I would respond, and we would high-five and take a picture.

Before my campaign, there was even a website called whoisandrewyang.com where different Andrew Yangs would write entries and post pictures about themselves, like we were all alternate versions of each other. I perused it out of curiosity but didn't include myself; I probably should have.

At the start of my presidential run, I bought the URL andrewyang.com, which was owned by a design professor in Illinois. He was a nice guy. I think we struck a deal for around five thousand dollars, which felt like a win. I hope he's now happy with what has happened to that website over these recent years. I hope, too, that the other Andrew Yangs are pleased generally. We were always hard to google. Even when I was the CEO of a company, the top Internet search result for *Andrew Yang* was a doll maker. The day I beat him in the results was a good day.

Anyway, part of me has some sympathy for this other Andrew Yang, if these poems are genuine. But most of me wants to set the record straight: THOSE ARE NOT MY POEMS. And there's only one way to prove it—demonstrate my literary skills. These are *my* poems:

A Poem by Andrew Yang (the real one)

Words.

Flowing out of my fingers on the laptop screen.

Sharing meaning.

With whom?

What version of myself shall fall on this page?

Which Andrew Yang?

There can be only one. Highlander. Jet Li.

But there are many.

The Happy Warrior.

By necessity, by design.

Because the world needs us to be.

How close did I come to naming one of my boys

    Andrew Yang Jr.?

Not close.

Doubt Evelyn would have gone for it.

Be their own people.

Out of many. One.

Out of one name, many.

Okay, that was fun. Let's keep going. Here's one on Universal Basic Income:

UBI

You and I.

So fly, so fly.

Help people feel like they can touch the sky.

Help people look each other in the eye.

You and I.

UBI.

So awesome. More!

"Hey Yang, Where's My Thousand Bucks?"

"I'm working on it."

MATH

US GDP was $29.35 trillion in 2024, $87,081 per person.

AI is going to make that much higher.

That seems like enough to give people $12,000.

Democracy

A fading dream.

Millions wonder, *Why are these my two choices in a land of 340 million?*

It's because our system does not reward or produce leaders.

Who can we trust?

The currents are too strong.

We mistrust those who swim alongside the market.

The political market, it demands a lot.

But if you go against it you are lost, never to be heard from again.

So the people rage and cry out.

Better to burn it down than be lied to or condescended
    to.
We cannot be placated or sedated or duped forever.
Where does this end?
Who is electable, and who decides?
Certainly not the people; they can't be trusted.
When faced with an ineffective, inhuman bureaucracy,
    the people will turn to those who make them feel
    something real.
Things can come apart faster than most realize.

Okay, that was way too heavy and dark. Time
to lighten it up.

Forward

340 million people.
Millions of different perspectives.
Only two parties?
Huh.

Lex and Rex

These are what I named my pecs.
"Lex" for left pec.
"Rex" for right pec.
I can make them "talk."
Or at least I could.
When I fed them regularly.

What did they eat?

Plates; but not plates of food.

Iron plates devoured while prone on a slightly smelly
   bench.

They ate several times a week.

Now they are diminished.

One can barely hear them.

They served their purpose.

Once they threatened the world, now they amuse
   children.

Evelyn told our kids that the other poems were mine. They believed her. Man, I'm terrible at poetry. I now pass the mic back to the other Andrew Yang, wherever he is. I hope he's out of the darkness now.

Chapter 27

Award Season

During COVID, I was on a Zoom that would change my life. It was with Nick Troiano, a guy who has dedicated his career to making democracy work better. He runs an organization called Unite America that fights for things like open primaries and ranked-choice voting. If you don't know what those things are, just know that they're good.

I asked him, "Who is the most prominent person for ranked-choice voting?"

He answered with two words that have haunted me ever since: "Probably you."

Shit. That's not what you want.

But then it kind of made sense, as anyone inside the system wouldn't push too hard for improving it. I resolved then to do a better job advocating for these issues; if I was the most prominent guy for them, I'd better pull my weight.

Fast-forward to mid-2022 and I was slated to get a Democracy Leader Award from Fairvote, a reform org I had joined the board of the prior year.

They were having a gala in New York to recognize me and a couple of other people.

In general, there are three kinds of awards one receives:

1. An award that gives you money. These are very rare, and thus treasured.
2. An award that does not give you money, but you go and talk (or, if you're lame, you record a video).
3. An award that requires you to talk *and* raise money. These are the most common.

This particular award was in category #3, which I was totally cool with because I loved the organization. For six years I'd been the head of Venture for America, which I had started back in 2011. I had tried to raise money without having a party and it didn't work. So eventually we held our own galas and started giving awards. And you know what those awardees had to do? Raise money for the org. I knew the drill.

So when you're in this position, you have a couple of choices for the gala:

1. Pay for a table yourself, and then invite friends who come for free; or
2. Invite rich friends for whom paying five hundred dollars a ticket will not

make them super pissed at you, either because they're really rich or they love the cause, or both.

For this event, I went with #2, which by the way is what the organization prefers because then they might have some new rich supporters who fall in love with the mission. Shout out to Joe Geraci and Dan Wisniewski, who love democracy! (They bought a table at the event.)

Then you get dressed up, show up, give a nice speech, and try to remind Evelyn why she married you. You also typically meet some other great people; one of the other award recipients was Kathryn Murdoch, who has spent millions trying to make voting work better to help address climate change.

If you're fortunate enough to receive an award, know that there's probably some work involved, but then that's probably why you're getting the award in the first place—so put on a smile and find your tux and get ready to bug some friends. And if your friend gets an award, show up and be a good sport about it. That's what makes the world go round.

Chapter 28

My Advice to Grads

In the spring of 2022, I got an email asking me to speak at Columbia Law School's graduation ceremony. It came from a high school classmate of mine, Jed Purdy, who was a professor at the law school.

I was immensely flattered and said yes pretty quickly. I then had to actually write a speech. What do you say that everyone hasn't already heard? I wanted to be as honest as possible. We've all seen and heard all of the graduation speeches. What could I contribute that wouldn't be the same old, same old?

A couple months later, on a rainy afternoon in upper Manhattan, I put on one of those cap-and-gown outfits and sat onstage waiting for my name to be called. It was a bit more imposing a situation than I'd imagined, primarily because there were parents as far as the eye could see, and parents of law school graduates are even older than ordinary parents. Also, for some reason my mom wanted to come, like a redo of my graduation when I'd said absolutely nothing.

Then I heard my cue: "Let's welcome Andrew Yang to return to his alma mater this afternoon. Thank you, Andrew, for being here today." I got up to shake the dean's hand, gestured to the crowd, and let out a big "Thank you!" I started the speech with some of my biographical highlights that I've already discussed, so I'll pick up near the end:

Columbia Graduation Speech (May 16, 2022)

What wisdom can one take from someone who has made objectively unwise career decisions repeatedly in his career?

I know where you're coming from. Law school graduates tend very strongly to be institutionalists. You've spent three years learning legal arguments and a degree of intellectual discipline. You are trained to be experts in rules, and rules require structures and institutions to support them. You will be recruited by high-resource firms and organizations that need smart people who can work hard. And yes, you also have certain expectations of your own careers and advancement and opportunities.

And yet, this is an era of institutional struggle. We can see it and feel it around us every day. For some of you, this is daunting and you look forward to getting into an environment where things make sense as long as you work hard and produce results. For others of you, you sense opportunities but don't quite know how to pursue them. And at the same time, you each have your own personal lives to figure out, as you come to a point when your life decisions begin to have import and weight.

My advice to you is threefold. First, ride this new Columbia Law degree for all it's worth. What does that mean? Now that you have a Columbia Law degree, people will assume that you're smart. That means, to truly maximize the value of this degree, you have to do some things that make people question whether you know what you're doing. Think about it: if you just did smart things from now on, then what is the point of this degree? You could have done smart things *without* the degree. Now that you have it, you have to make use of it. Think of it as having a "Get Out of Jail Free" card for the rest of your career.

Now, some parents here are groaning at this—you thought those days were over. Well, my mom is here to tell you those days are never over. They go on forever. But if your child plays it right, they too can be the twenty-fifth most well-regarded political figure in all the land.

Second, find a problem that you can work on for years and feel good about dedicating your time to. It could be a market-based problem. It could be trying to improve treatment for a particular group. Right now, I'm pursuing two related problems: alleviating poverty and reforming our democracy. These are very big projects that I can work on for years and feel good about.

Right now, you might not know what drives or animates you. That's fine. When I was your age, the problem I was most consumed with was getting a date. I never did solve that problem until seven years later when I met Evelyn. You can just do good work on what is in front of you while you wait, but keep an eye on what you find yourself reading about and caring about. One of the enormous virtues of your new Columbia Law degree is that, if you show up on someone's doorstep saying, "I want to work with you to help solve the problem you're working on," they will be THRILLED to accept your help. And I can say with total confidence that if it's a significant problem, someone is working on it right now. Indeed, perhaps the greatest challenge that lies ahead is actually figuring out what you care about, because this process typically takes years and evolves over time, and the market will try to hide it from you, not show it to you. So lie in wait for it. Stay the person who cares about important problems and can show up on someone's doorstep and say, "I'm here to help."

And that leaves me with the highest ambition—have confidence that you can do what you want and make the market follow you. What do I mean? Most all of you were recruited by firms with big budgets as second-years and are going off to work for them after graduation. That's fine. I did it too. That is the market for people like you. But eventually, you may find yourself in a position where you want to do something, but the market doesn't exist yet. Know that if you work hard, you can create that market for yourself. When I ran for president, no one knew whether there was a demand for a candidate running on an idea like Universal Basic Income. I thought it existed, but I needed to work hard to find out. It took time. Now I'm looking to do the same for a new, independent approach to politics and measures like ranked-choice voting. There will be times in your career where you'll do what the market wants you to do, and there will be times when you're going to have to stand up and go against it. But if you push in a certain direction that you care deeply about and work hard enough, the market will follow you. It will spring up around you. People will reach out to help you. It's the best feeling in the world when it happens. You form lifelong relationships. And the more of you who have that feeling, the better off our world will be.

What's funny is that this market I'm describing is really the people around you right now. You'll each receive a call or message from a classmate at some point in the future saying, "Hey, I'm going to run for office," or, "I'm going to start this new initiative." When you get that message, do what you can to help. We all have a role to play. If you're on the inside of an organization, lend a hand, gather some people together, and invest some resources. We don't all have to quit our jobs, but we do have to support the person who is trying to discover if good people care enough to move us forward.

So those are the three guideposts I have for you—make the most of your degree by testing people's belief that you know what you're doing, find a problem to solve that's significant enough that you'll care about solving it each day, and have confidence that if you do what you want and work hard at it, the market will follow you—not the other way around.

It's no exaggeration to say that the future of civilization may rest on the choices you all make. Find that voice inside you, apply yourself with the same energy you have to reaching your goals thus far, and I have no doubt that you'll do great.

Congratulations, Columbia Law School Class of '22! Let's do all we can with what we've been given and build a future we'll be proud to pass on.

∽◎∼

My comments were met with warm applause. Jed texted me, *Well given, well received.* More importantly, my mom was happy. She and Evelyn greeted me afterward and we went off into the night to get some dinner.

Chapter 29

Shane Gillis

Back when I was running for president, a comedian named Shane Gillis was in danger of being fired from *Saturday Night Live* the week he was supposed to be announced as joining the cast. His offense? He called me a "Jew Chink" among other jokes on a comedy podcast that no one had actually listened to.

I had never heard of Shane Gillis. When I caught wind of the situation he was facing, I sat down to watch some of his comedy clips with Evelyn. After seeing him perform in a variety of settings, I concluded that Shane wasn't nasty, malignant, or racist. He was . . . a comedian.

I'm generally in the camp that artists should be given very wide discretion, and that trying to cancel someone's job or livelihood is often totally out of proportion with the offense. I tweeted at the time, *Shane—I prefer comedy that makes people think . . .* I also added, *For the record, I do not think he should lose his job.* I figured that as the aggrieved party, maybe my saying something would influence matters.

It didn't; Shane was indeed fired from *SNL*. He and I had a call during this time, which helped affirm that I had done the right thing, as he wasn't defensive or angry in the least. He seemed shell-shocked and like he was processing it all.

A few years later, Shane had amassed a much bigger following as a comedian via YouTube and touring. What impressed me was that he seemed like he had avoided the path of least resistance; a natural lane for him would have been to become "anti-woke" or something along those lines, but he actively seemed to be dodging that. He never wanted to talk about being canceled. I was curious, so I pinged him and asked if he'd come on my podcast to talk about his journey.

Shane and I sat down in mid-2022. I shared with him that I had been called "gook" and various epithets growing up, and that those hurt at the time, but we were also all idiot kids ribbing each other over whatever we could identify. Shane related that he just wanted to figure out what was funny, and that he wanted everything to revolve around that and nothing else. He reminded me of a lot of the guys I grew up with. We both enjoyed the conversation, which was viewed almost one million times on YouTube, and agreed to stay in touch.

* * *

The next month, I was in San Francisco and Shane was performing at Cobb's Comedy Club, a venue where I had given a book talk just a few months before. I texted Shane to see if I could come by with Evelyn and some friends. He said, "Sure!"

I told him I had one request: "I want to introduce you."

"Sure, sounds good."

I arrived and met up with Shane in the green room upstairs, which was not fancy. Shane was watching a basketball game and having a beer with a couple other local comics. We shot the shit and talked about the game. Eventually, I went on after the other comics. What's fun was that I just came onstage unannounced. Pretty quickly, the crowd recognized me. I had on the usual blue blazer and dark jeans combination from the trail, so I guess I looked like myself.

I wasn't sure what the reaction would be, but it was a ton of hooting and hollering; the Bay Area and I have a special connection. I had to pause to wait for the applause to die down.

"It's great to be here with you all tonight. Shane couldn't be here, so he sent me as his last-minute replacement . . ."

Some light laughter.

". . . because he loves Asians. More than any other kind of person."

People laughed harder.

"I first met Shane when I was running for president of the United States."

Applause.

"He was trying to join the cast of *SNL*. And we both fell short. But Shane went on to become one of the most beloved comics in the entire country. And I . . . I went on to introduce Shane.

"I don't live here, but the media introduced me as California tech billionaire Andrew Yang when I was running for president. Remember that? And my wife who's here tonight was like, 'Where the fuck is this billion dollars? And why am I driving a Subaru?'"

Evelyn screamed from the crowd at this point.

"In all seriousness, it's been a long few years. You've been through a lot, I've been through a lot. Shane's been through a lot. But through everything, Shane has kept his spirit, stayed true to himself, honed his craft, and become a better human being and a better comedian—am I right, San Francisco?"

Rousing applause.

"And so, it is my pleasure to introduce to you all my running mate for 2024, the people's champ, Shane Gillis!"

Shane came out and we dapped it up.

Less than two years later, Shane was invited to host *SNL* in New York. I talked to him afterward—it was clear he felt like he'd closed a book about four and a half years after his initial firing. It was a true full-circle American redemption arc. He had won the old-fashioned way: by being himself, working hard, and winning people over with his talent and craft. We should all be so fortunate.

Chapter 30

Whatever, It's Cool

My two boys are twelve and nine as I'm writing this. They are not what you'd call rugged.

My older son, Christopher, is on the autism spectrum. Ever since I can remember, he would react very strongly or emotionally to his environment. The texture of the ground, the temperature of water; small stimuli would have him screaming bloody murder. It was very stressful to be around.

Today, after years of intervention and individual attention, he is more balanced but he still becomes very anxious about the passage of time or a change in schedule or environment. He will react very negatively by saying, "It's too late!" or, "Going there will take too long!" His knee-jerk reaction is to express concern.

His younger brother, Damian, is more at ease with his surroundings. He likes to stay up late and play with foam swords from LegoLand. Damian has a strong tendency to jump off beds or sofas, often banging a knee or elbow. Given that he is the sole cause of the mishap, you would think he might take it in stride.

You'd be wrong. Damian treats any knock or nick as a calamity, crying for his mom as if he's been mauled by a bear.

I have tried my best to get both of my boys to respond with aplomb, or at least fake it. I remember being quite sensitive as a young boy. I was a bit of a crybaby. But in my adolescence, I became more of a stoic, particularly when it came to physical pain. I remember one kid challenging me and kicking me hard in the shins. I looked at him as if he hadn't done anything. He freaked out and ran off.

So for my boys, when they are upset, I tell them there are three magic words that make everything feel better: *Whatever, it's cool.*

When Christopher freaks out about an unexpected trip outside the house, I admonish him, "Whatever, it's cool." Until he repeats the words, like a mantra. When Damian cries about bonking his head, I intone to him, "Whatever, it's cool." He will say it through tears.

Does it help? Does it make them feel better? It seems like it.

Some people will likely object to this, that I'm somehow conditioning my boys to ignore their very real pain or emotion. That it will turn them into unfeeling automatons or men who are not in touch with their emotions. My response to this is: You have never met my boys. They are whiny. It is unappealing. After an episode or two, you would be begging for them to say, "Whatever, it's cool."

Evelyn is a very doting and attentive mom. I appreciate it a great deal. I once asked my kids, "Would you describe yourselves as mama's boys?"

"Yes!" they both exclaimed proudly and quickly.

They sometimes take Evelyn a bit for granted. I find it very aggravating. I have said to them, "Boys, appreciate everything your mom does for you, because if it were up to Dad, you would be eating bread and butter every day, because that's all I know how to make." They often call out for Mom to help them out or find something for them. When I was growing up, I was often left to my own devices because my parents were at work.

One day I said to them, "Boys, if your mom weren't here, you know who Dad would have help you with things that you can figure out how to do yourselves? Inflato."

"Who's Inflato?"

"Inflato is a balloon man Dad would blow up and put in the living room, like outside a used-car lot. And you would say, *Inflato, can you get me something to drink?* And you know what Inflato would say back to you?"

"Nothing?"

"That's right. Because Inflato can't talk. And then you'd go do it yourself."

Both my boys find this very funny. Now they

yell "Inflato!" anytime they know I'm about to say "Do it yourself," which is quite often.

Another argument I make to them when they are being whiny or negative is that they wouldn't exist if I was like that. "Boys, you have to be more upbeat and resilient. Your mom never would have agreed to go out with me if I was complaining all the time. The main thing she liked about me is that she could eat my food and I wouldn't say a word. If I whined like you, she would never have dated me or agreed to marry me. Then you wouldn't exist. Instead, Mom would have married a dermatologist named Dr. Neil Gupta. Then you would be Zach and Lance Gupta. Is that what you want?"

They both find this very funny too. "Dad, I wouldn't mind being Lance Gupta. That's a cool name."

"Well, even if you'd be happy, Dad would be sad because I'd be all alone. So be more positive."

When Evelyn isn't around, I sometimes say, "Well, it's just us, the Three Amibros! Quick, what's the amibro greeting?" We then do our secret handshake. If this were a movie, that would be key to distinguishing me from my AI replacement.

Most importantly, I've told them that if they ever see Evelyn with another guy, they should yell, "You're not my dad! I hate you!" You have to train them to be the next line of defense, in case you leave an opening. You might do something stupid, or leave for months on end to run for president.

Chapter 31
Bro-djacent

In early 2022, I tweeted a thread about how American men weren't doing so well by the numbers. An editor from the *Washington Post* reached out and asked me to write an op-ed on the topic.

"Sure," I said. Writing an op-ed is sometimes a good opportunity to get a message out. And this was a topic near and dear to my heart. Here it is:

The Boys Are Not All Right

Here is one of the biggest problems facing America: boys and men across all regions and ethnic groups have been failing, both absolutely and relatively, for years. This is catastrophic for our country.

The data are clear. Boys are more than twice as likely as girls to be diagnosed with attention-deficit/hyperactivity disorder, according to the Centers for Disease Control and Prevention; are five times as likely to spend time in juvenile detention; and are less likely to finish high school.

Unfortunately, it doesn't get better when boys become adults. Men now make up only 40.5 percent of college students. Male community college enrollment declined by 14.7 percent in 2020 alone, compared with 6.8 percent for women. Median wages for men have declined since 1990 in real terms. Roughly one-third of men are either unemployed or out of the workforce. More US men ages eighteen to thirty-four are now living with their parents than with romantic partners.

Economic transformation has been a big contributor. More than two-thirds of manufacturing workers are men; the sector has lost more than five million jobs since 2000. That's a lot of unemployed men. Not just coincidentally, "deaths of despair"—those caused by suicide, overdose, and alcoholism—have surged to unprecedented levels among middle-aged men over the past twenty years.

Research shows that one significant factor women look for in a partner is a steady job. As men's unemployment rises, their romantic prospects decline. Unsurprisingly, according to a Pew Research Center analysis of data from 1960 to 2010, the proportion of adults without a college degree who marry plummeted from just over 70 percent to roughly 45 percent.

Many boys are thus often growing up raised by single mothers, the share more than doubling between 1980 and 2019, from 18 percent to 40 percent. A study from 2015 found that "as more boys grow up without their father in the home, and as women . . . are viewed as the more stable achievers, boys and girls alike [may] come to see males as having a lower achievement orientation . . . College becomes something that many girls, but only some boys, do."

Yes, men have long had societal advantages over women and in some ways continue to be treated favorably. But male achievement—alongside that of women— is a condition for a healthy society. And male failure begets male failure, to society's detriment. Our media, institutions, and public leadership have failed to address this crisis, framing boys and men as the problem themselves rather than as people requiring help.

This needs to change. Helping boys and men succeed should be a priority for all our society's institutions. Schools that have succeeded in keeping boys on track should be expanded, by both increasing the number of students they serve and exporting their methods to other schools. Vocational education and opportunities should be redoubled; the nation's public school system should start the process for early age groups, and apprenticeship programs should be supported by the federal government. Nonprofits helping boys and men—such as Big Brothers Big Sisters of America and the YMCA—should receive more investment.

Resources that keep families together when they want to stay together, such as marriage counseling, should be subsidized by the government—a much more cost-efficient approach than dealing with the downstream effects. The enhanced child tax credit should be renewed, helping stabilize families.

Drives for national service and contribution, such as an American Exchange Program or national service years, should be resuscitated. And businesses and industries that employ large numbers of men, such as manufacturing, should be invested in and reinvigorated.

On a cultural level, we must stop defining masculinity as necessarily toxic and start promoting positive masculinity. Strong, healthy, fulfilled men are more likely to treat women well.

The above is, of course, a prodigious undertaking. But I see the need around me all the time.

A number of my friends have become detached from society. Everyone hits a snag at some point—losing a job, facing a divorce—but my male friends seem less able to bounce back. Male dysfunction tends to take on an air of nihilism and dropping out. As a society, we don't provide many avenues for healthy recovery.

Here's the simple truth I've heard from many men: we need to be needed. We imagine ourselves as builders, soldiers, workers, brothers—part of something bigger than ourselves. We deal with idleness terribly.

"A man . . . with no means of filling up time," George Orwell wrote, is "as miserable out of work as a dog on the chain." Left to our own devices, many of us will fail. And from our failure, terrible things result for the country, well beyond any individual self-destruction.

⤜⧟⤛

A little dark, I know. The op-ed was mentioned on major news programs for the week. *Morning Joe* ran the piece with commentary. Bill Maher had me on to discuss it. On some level, people really wanted to talk about the topic.

But there was also an odd backlash—I got accused of being pro-men at the expense of women. Of being a bro, essentially.

I don't think it's a zero-sum game. You can help women and men at the same time. I don't think the "Aargh, take it all back and dominate! Hulk Smash!!" message from the right is very productive. But I do think we should be doing a lot more for men and boys from a societal perspective.

It would help everyone, in part because American men are somewhat aggressive by nature, and that aggression travels. If you think about how the nation got started, who the heck picks up and sails across the ocean to a new land to set up shop? Who would go to another continent and enslave millions of people to work the fields? Who moves west to take over vacant land and kicks out or murders anyone who stands in the way? You'd have to be kind of aggro. U-S-A!!!

We're extraordinarily militaristic. The US has almost eight hundred military bases around the world, on every continent. There are another four hundred and fifty military bases in the United States, with all fifty states having at least one. We are the only people who are obsessed with American football, which if you think about it is sort of a brutal war game over dominating a patch of land. My least favorite team? The Patriots. I'm enjoying their down era.

Relatedly, we love guns. Lots and lots of guns.

Look, I'm not cosigning all of the testosterone flowing through this country. The point is that we have a lot of anger and energy that's going to find its way somewhere or other. When I was running for president, I said we should set up MMA gyms everywhere and have a national tournament at every age and weight, have the toughest men and women in the country duke it out. Better to channel the anger into something productive like figuring out which state has the most ass-kickers than let it find other pursuits.

Knuckleheads will fight. Tyler Cowen calls it "the Bad Men problem." But just as there's violence and toxic masculinity, there's also positive and heroic masculinity. Men imagine ourselves to be kings, warriors, CEOs, athletes, ladies' men, geniuses, soldiers, workers, achievers, and part of a band of brothers. That can lead to noxious behavior. It can also lead to running into a burning building to save someone or sacrificing your own interests for the good of a team or a country.

Boys and men are shaped by organizations and environments. We all know people who got whipped into shape by being in a structured setting, whether a military boot camp or boarding school or jiujitsu dojo or even their family. On the flip side, men deal with idleness terribly, as I mentioned in the op-ed. Unemployed men volunteer less than employed men, despite having a lot more time on our hands. What do we do with all of that time? "Computer use" shoots up. So do drinking and gambling. Shocking, I know.

By the way, the takeover of online sports gambling in all of our sports programming is AWFUL for men. You can't turn on ESPN without being bombarded by bets you should make. I'm someone who uses gambling apps, so I know they are bad news. For every dollar spent on betting, men save two dollars less in actual investment accounts. Bankruptcies go up. Domestic violence goes up. So do anxiety and depression.

Have I had my evening ruined by a failed parlay? Yes, I have. I should never have believed in that bum. Happily, I didn't do anything stupid afterward.

Betting on sports online is a perfect storm for men because it combines a bunch of things many of us love: sports, money, speed, risk, and thinking that we know something that others don't. It feels like a faux job in that it will pay you money for time spent, but it could also cost you your savings, your relationships, and your mental health.

By the way, women in general don't deal with idleness poorly at all, perhaps because they're rarely actually idle. You know what unemployed women are much more likely to do? Volunteer or go back to school.

Men like to feel like we are needed, productive, and/or gaining ground. I tried a bunch of stuff in my twenties that didn't really work. The self-doubt gnawed at me. When things started to click in my thirties, it helped straighten me out. Feeling valued or connected made me a better person. A better man. I want that for as many people as possible. Good men will be better for everyone.

There are a few people who have been making the case for boys and men in a nonreactionary way: Scott Galloway, Richard V. Reeves, Liz Plank, Jonathan Haidt, Lisa Britton, Bill Maher, and Warren Farrell, to name a few. Somehow I've made the list of sane people who think we should be doing more. I welcome it.

Having two young boys at home, I see it all of the time. They could be great. They could be terrible. It depends on a lot of things. Right now they want to be YouTubers. Don't worry, I'm working on it.

Chapter 32

SBF, Elizabeth Holmes, and Me

In August of 2022, I was invited to a book party in Manhattan hosted by Sam Bankman-Fried. I had never met Sam before and was interested in attending. After all, this guy was worth a bazillion dollars and his company FTX had its name on billboards and an NBA arena.

It was held in a private event space near Madison Park, one of those mysterious spots you'd never know existed. There were two members of Congress present and at least one other billionaire. It was a small event, maybe twenty-five people. We stood and made small talk as staff served us cocktails from a nearby open bar.

Sam showed up, and as the host, everyone went to greet him. I shook his hand and thanked him for inviting me. He acknowledged me awkwardly. I was surprised by his appearance. Sam had on a white T-shirt that seemed like it hadn't been washed in a while. His hair was unkempt. He hadn't shaved. He was also a little bit puffy. It felt like he had spent the past few days on a beanbag playing video games and eating pizza.

We sat down for dinner at a dramatic rectangular table and introduced ourselves. People had interesting careers: one was a Hollywood producer; another was a social scientist; the author of the book was there—it was about how we owed generations in the future a lot more than we think since there will presumably be many more people. He said a few words and invited questions.

Now, in these kinds of environments, I feel some pressure to say something intelligent or profound. After all, I have a reputation to uphold. But instead of something deep about humanity's future, I asked the question that was at the tip of my tongue: "Hey, are there actually copies of the book here? Because I'd love to get one signed."

My question evoked confusion. The author glanced at Sam. Sam blinked and turned to one of his staffers. The staffer seemed to be looking at me.

"Oh, it's fine," I quickly added, "we can totally order copies online. Probably better that way." I didn't want to seem ungrateful or discourteous given that we were all sitting there eating a fancy meal as guests. Everyone else quickly followed suit and changed the subject.

But still, it was odd. Who hosts a book party for an author and forgets to bring the books?

I've been around a number of billionaires and CEO types, and nine times out of ten there's a hyper-competent person standing around who is making sure that things that are supposed to happen actually happen. I got the distinct sense that Sam did not have one of those people.

We continued a lovely evening. Dessert was served. One of the members of Congress said to me, "We should get lunch together sometime soon." I got a picture of several of us at dinner, but some instinct told me to not post it.

When I got home, Evelyn asked me about the event.

"It was nice. But a little odd."

Sam would be arrested for fraud in the Bahamas four months later. Sure glad I never posted that picture! Sam wasn't the first famous fraudster I've met. The other is probably even more infamous—Elizabeth Holmes of Theranos, a blood test start-up.

Elizabeth and I met at the White House of all places. We were both Presidential Ambassadors of Global Entrepreneurship in 2015. I was the token Asian. When we met in the hallway before going in to meet the president, she took my hand in what seemed like an exaggeratedly firm handshake and said in a deep voice while staring at me, "Hello, I'm Elizabeth." She was wearing eye makeup and a black turtleneck.

"Hello, I'm Andrew. Nice to meet you," I replied. *She seems strange*, I thought to myself. I had heard of her of course—she was the youngest female self-made billionaire at the time and had been on the cover of *Fortune* and other magazines. We were at the White House, so you have to assume everyone is pretty legit.

But something didn't fit. There was something off. I drifted away and spent most of the day with other ambassadors like Daniel Lubetzky, who had a secret stash of KIND bars.

Elizabeth would be accused of fraud later that year. *Huh*, I thought when I heard the news. *Maybe that was what was activating my Spidey sense.*

Most successful entrepreneurs and executives that I meet have a certain energy to them. Sometimes it's quiet and reserved. Other times it's a little more in-your-face. It's a confidence that they can make things happen because they've made big things happen before. They're unlikely to get fazed, because they've been through the wringer and come out the other side successfully. You get a version of the same vibe from experienced fighters and military personnel.

I did not get that vibe from Elizabeth Holmes, even in our brief exchange. It felt like an affectation or role-playing. I didn't get that vibe from Sam Bankman-Fried either; he felt like a slob.

Now, in neither case did I do anything other than express my impressions to Evelyn. With

Elizabeth, I kept my mouth shut in part because she was a role model to women entrepreneurs at the time, and even I thought, *Maybe it's in my head because she's so unusual.* With Sam, it was a private event that most people didn't even know happened. Plus, what are you going to do, say, "Hey, I think this person seemed fishy"? No one would invite you to anything ever again.

What's the lesson here? I'm not sure other than that sometimes it's possible to be a fraudster because it's in no one's interest to dig or say anything. The party and conference circuit are kind of a go-along-and-get-along scene. The more people around, the more legit it all seems, and the less likely someone who comes will want to be a jackass.

Also, if you're going to host a book party, bring books.

Chapter 33
Famous People

"You know a lot of famous people," an old friend once observed. "Any stories to tell?"

I probably do, but talking about it can make me feel like a jerk. So . . . what can I say? A lot of people are nice. Jon Hamm is very, very handsome in real life.

There are a few ways one meets celebrities if you're a guy like me. It could be in the course of work. It could be by chance because you're at the same event. It also could be via personal activity.

A couple years ago, I spoke at the Schwarzenegger Institute at USC about improving politics. After my talk for a few hundred students, a member of Arnold Schwarzenegger's staff came up to me and said, "Great talk! The governor would like you to come by his house afterward."

I responded, "Wonderful, I'd be glad to." To myself, I'm thinking, *I'm going to meet the Terminator!*

An hour later, we roll into his house, which is

obviously quite nice but nothing as spectacular as one might imagine. We headed to the patio in the back, where Arnold was chilling with some friends. He got up and greeted me. "Ahn-drew, well-come. The wook you're doo-ing is soh im-POH-tahnt," he said, sounding exactly like himself. Looking him in the eye, I couldn't help but smile broadly. But then, I noticed his friend, and I got even more excited. It was Ralf Moeller, who was the bad guy in *Best of the Best II*. I started quoting Ralf's lines back to him and everyone was very entertained because I was geeking out with Arnold's much more obscure buddy.

We sat and talked politics for a while. We agreed to try to do more together. Toward the end, Arnold and I reenacted the *Predator* handshake.

As an eighties kid, this was such a thrill.

* * *

Occasionally, you run into someone whom you've had an online interaction with that wasn't necessarily pleasant. Like Henry Golding, the star of *Crazy Rich Asians*. He once called me a "twat" on Twitter, which I didn't think much of because it was in response to a campaign tweet. He was a high-class guy when I met him in person at a charity event, and we hashed it out and took a nice photo together. I joked with Evelyn afterward, "I should post this photo and say, *Look at this twat.*" But I would never do that—again, Henry seemed like a great guy!

Another reason I wouldn't share that photo is because it's obnoxious to post a shot with a celebrity when you're involved in politics, unless they're into it. I took a picture with Channing Tatum when I met him at a charity event in Alabama, and someone nearby said, "Careful, Channing, you just endorsed him for president." Channing, cool as a cucumber, responded, "No problem. We need something new." Did I mention Channing Tatum is a cool guy? He had a learning disability growing up and is extraordinarily empathetic as a result.

Sometimes the kids are there, which can make things interesting. My family met Emma Watson at a conference in Colorado. My older son, who as I've mentioned is autistic, knows her primarily as Hermione in the *Harry Potter* movies. Upon seeing her, Christopher blurted out, "You look older—when were you less old?"

She smirked, taken aback. "I'm not sure."

Evelyn, trying to smooth it over, said, "Yesterday. Everyone was less old yesterday."

Christopher kept evaluating Emma. "You look older."

One time on the road at another conference, I went to a nightclub. There was a booth with a couple of massive security guys guarding it—they were so big you couldn't see who was at the table. Of course I got curious, so I walked up.

One of the security guys—an imposing black guy—recognized me immediately. "Yooooo . . . Yang!" He nodded, stood aside, and motioned for me to walk on by and sit down. There at the booth were Katy Perry and Orlando Bloom. Orlando saw me and smiled and stood up to greet me. That happens sometimes. He's a handsome, rugged guy in his forties. We talked for a little while, and the only thing I kept thinking looking at him was, *It's Legolas! You're Legolas from* Lord of the Rings! *Say, "And you have my bow."*

Katy was also very friendly, including to a friend of mine who was a bit starstruck. "Hi, I'm Katy! What's your name?" Needless to say, my friend became an even bigger fan in that moment.

Regarding celebrities, one of the questions I often hear is, "Who's an asshole?" The truth is that most everyone is very pleasant. For better or worse, there's a little bit of a bond between celebrities in that you're generally inclined to be nice to each other. Everyone has a journey they're traveling and everyone has been through some level of nonsense.

It's true for most of the talk show hosts, as you'd expect. Stephen Colbert. Seth Meyers. Jimmy Kimmel. Ellen DeGeneres was kind to me in person. Jimmy and I compared notes on how to beat Ted Cruz in basketball. I'm sad that that game never came to pass.

My favorite celebrity meeting? It goes back to my adolescence. If you'll remember, one of my favorite bands growing up was the Cure. Robert Smith and I became friendly online during the campaign. When he came to Madison Square Garden a couple years later, I reached out to see if we could meet. He said, "Definitely, would love that!" and gave me the information for his tour manager.

A few weeks later, I would accompany my childhood friends Miika and Andy to see Robert Smith and the Cure backstage at MSG. It was a long way from buying cheap tickets to see him way back in the nineties.

Robert was lovely: "I'm so glad you like my music."

"Are you kidding? Who doesn't? We are thrilled to be here!"

Being able to go full circle with one of my teenage idols was incredible. You know how they say, "Never meet your heroes"? Nah. I actually highly recommend it.

And the concert was amazing too. Evelyn said, "I felt transported to another time." Robert's still got it. Better than ever.

Part V

SAVING DEMOCRACY—IT'S GOING GREAT!

Chapter 34

Forward

In October of 2021, I kicked off the Forward Party. It accompanied a book and a tour that took me all over the country. I insisted on putting Des Moines on the tour just to visit my old stomping grounds.

As you'd imagine, this wound up connecting me with people who had also concluded that a new direction was necessary for American politics. One of them was Christie Todd Whitman, the former governor of New Jersey who had written a book called *It's My Party Too*. She joked that if she had to write a sequel today, it would be called *No, It Isn't*.

Christie was on the board of the Renew America Movement (RAM), a group that was trying to fight the extremes in the Republican Party. Alongside them was the similarly named Serve America Movement (SAM), which was working on a new political party. We sat around a conference room in New York asking each other, "How are we going to work together?" I said, "Look, what we're trying to do is regarded by most people as impossible. It's going to stay that way if we all try to do it separately. If we all get together, we'd have a chance." After a series of meetings, we decided to join forces.

Of course, that's much easier said than done— these were three separate organizations with different CEOs and boards and teams of staffers and budgets. Anyone who has been around the block knows that mergers are very tricky endeavors— and they usually only involve two companies, not three. Still, I was of the opinion that we had to find a way. We were trying to do the impossible, after all, so we might as well start with the extremely difficult.

The problems came early. The day before the merger, our chosen CEO notified us that he wasn't going to be able to stay on because the TV network that employed him—MSNBC—told him they wouldn't renew his contract if he worked for a new political party. That felt familiar; the same thing had happened to me at CNN. This threw the whole team-up into question.

I got on a call with the other orgs and said, "We are making this happen, no matter what." I pushed for a co-CEO arrangement that would keep everyone at the table. Happily, the other stakeholders realized that if we didn't make it happen now, the whole thing was going to fall apart.

We finally got through the bulk of the logistics around the merger, which was announced on July 27, 2022, and received an enormous amount of media coverage. I coauthored an op-ed in the *Washington Post* making the announcement that a new party was on the scene. The news was carried everywhere and our website got hundreds of thousands of visits.

Meanwhile, behind the scenes we were still sorting out some details with the merger. We had taken board members from each of the three organizations and glued them together into one mega-board. I started calling it the "Frankenboard," like Frankenstein's monster. We were still getting to know each other and trying to get along. The result was a lot of trying not to step on each others' toes.

After a few months, one of the co-CEOs withdrew and we put out a national search for a new CEO. This landed Lindsey Drath, an executive from Unite America who had been working on democracy reform for years. She has been a breath of fresh air. And the board has gotten to know each other and turned a few people over while getting some new members.

I joke with people that I'm the cofounder of the third biggest political party, by resources, in the country, which isn't saying a whole lot; it just means we've outraised the Greens and the Libertarians, which isn't THAT hard. Our goal is to reform the political system so more people can vote for who they want, and to improve the incentives so that policymakers actually have to listen to the general public as opposed to just their party's base.

When many Americans hear "third party," they think of Ralph Nader screwing things up. At Forward, we are focused on the 500,000+ local races around the country, most of which don't have any meaningful competition. We're the smart, pragmatic, ground-up crew, as opposed to the failed "let's only concentrate on the presidential race" approach. We avoid being spoilers because that is impractical and we're trying to *improve* outcomes.

There have been pluses and minuses to the "let's work together" vibe of the Forward Party. One positive is that you attract great people who also want everyone to get together and focus on solutions. We have fifty-three elected officials who are now affiliated with Forward, from mayors to state senators to a member of Congress from North Carolina and even a US senator. There are more on the way; a lot of people are increasingly frustrated with the status quo. We have outstanding leaders and volunteers across the country and a mailing list of over 200,000.

Another plus is that, having walked the walk, we have been able to make a great case to Independents that they can join and have a seat at the table. The Independence Party of South Carolina changed its name to Forward and became our affiliate in that state, where I've spent a lot of time. The same thing happened in Utah and Minnesota.

One downside is that people are often drawn to conflict. Where's the drama in fixing our voting system? I sometimes joke that we should have an extreme anti-extremist event. "Burn down the extremes! Aaaaargh!!!"

Fifty percent of Americans now say they're Independents; that's rising all the time, and there's an even higher rate among young people. The wind is at our backs—the question is how to build a fleet of boats strong enough to cross turbulent seas. But the journey has to be made. Or else we'll all be in the soup.

Chapter 35

Dean Phillips

I first met Minnesota congressman Dean Phillips at an event in DC in late 2022. It was a campaign finance reform event hosted by the organization American Promise. Dean gave a speech basically saying, "I'm the only member who doesn't dial for dollars. That's not why the voters sent me here." I liked him immediately. We also both went to Brown University, and I tend to like fellow alums, who are often somewhat impractical and seldom jerks.

A few months later we met up in New York. He was deeply concerned that Joe Biden was a weak nominee and was considering running for president himself to kick off a competitive primary. As you'd imagine, I said, "Yes! Doooo it!!!!" So when Dean decided to actually run in October 2023, I figured I had to go in all the way and help. I thought that his case was correct—that running an eighty-one-year-old unpopular incumbent was somewhere between stupid and irresponsible—

and that a competitive primary would allow better candidates to emerge.

I converted my little squad into an impromptu Dean Phillips machine. Dean, to his credit, spent five million dollars of his own to set up a campaign. Zach Graumann met up with Dean in New Hampshire and signed on as his co–campaign manager. My newsletter with its audience of several hundred thousand became the Dean Phillips show, along with a lot of my social media accounts. I also co-hosted a fundraiser for him in New York with some friends and introduced him to various journalists.

I went up to Hanover, New Hampshire, in January 2024 to endorse Dean ahead of the first primary votes. Here is what I said:

> Hello, New Hampshire, it's great to be back! I went to high school here in the state and am going to speak at my alma mater tomorrow morning. And, of course, I spent months here campaigning four years ago and had a wonderful time.
>
> The last four years have not been great. This is a difficult and trying time. Americans across the country are questioning whether our future will be brighter than our past. Looming over this is our presidential race. Joe Biden has been an accomplished and substantial president. I endorsed him and voted for him in 2020

and was even a campaign surrogate. I've had the opportunity to meet and spend time with him and he is a good man, a true public servant, and a great American.

While he was the right candidate four years ago, he is not now. Four years ago, the Patriots were 12–4 and first in the AFC East. 2024 is not 2020.

President Biden said in 2020 that he was going to be the bridge to the next generation. Today, that is exactly what we need. Joe Biden is at 38 percent approval, a historic low and a full ten points lower than Barack Obama was at the same time. He is down by four in Wisconsin, down by eight in Georgia, and down by eight in Michigan, all swing states that Joe won in 2020. He is down by nine in North Carolina, virtually tied in Minnesota; I could go on and on.

There are people who say that Joe Biden has been down before and that he can win again. There are a number of reasons to think this optimism is misplaced. First, the Biden campaign already spent $25 million on advertising in the swing states trying to bump up the president's numbers by making people feel better about the economy. The impact? Zero. People have made up their minds about this economy and this president, and an ad campaign will not fix this.

Second, the president is eighty-one. All of the things that a candidate must do to be successful—travel, project energy, rally, meet voters, conduct interviews, call surrogates—all of them will be more difficult with an older candidate whose team will be concerned about him stumbling, literally or figuratively, at every turn. The candidate matters! It will be hard to reinvent Grandpa.

Third, this campaign is undermining the president's greatest strength. What is Joe's superpower? It is that he is a good man who many of us believe will try to do the right thing for the country. He is failing the George Washington test that he referenced recently in his Valley Forge speech— knowing when to pass the baton and walk away. His spirit of service has become ego and stubbornness that are leading us toward disaster. Sometimes, the highest form of leadership is stepping aside.

In a time of deep distress against Trump, the wrong plan is to run a terribly unpopular eighty-one-year-old incumbent who is down in polls both nationally and in the swing states that matter.

Why hasn't Joe gotten more competition? Here's why. Joe Biden appointed Jaime Harrison of South Carolina the chair of the DNC. There are only two decisionmakers here—Joe Biden and the man he appointed. Everyone else has been told to fall in line, and they are doing so even as it is leading us toward a second disastrous, calamitous loss to Donald Trump.

New Hampshire understands this self-dealing, as you are being punished right now by the DNC for holding a primary that you are required to hold by state law. You don't control the state legislature and couldn't make the change even if you wanted to. And this is a swing state! The DNC is failing the voters of this state and failing the country by stifling any competition, including canceling the primaries altogether in Florida and North Carolina, another swing state. They talk about championing democracy while crushing it just when we need it most.

For Gavin Newsom, Gretchen Whitmer, JB Pritzker, and other prominent Democrats, you are missing your moment. The country needs you now, not in 2028. If Trump wins in November, what will be left for us in 2028? What matters more, your standing in the party or your country? We all know you want to run for president, and your time is right now. In 2028, you'll also have Josh Shapiro and Wes Moore to contend with, and they won't have missed their moment.

In this time of need, only one man decided to place his country over his political career, put his own conviction above the chattering class, and that is the man I am proud to endorse as the next president of the United States, three-term congressman from Minnesota Dean Phillips!!!

Dean has the character, vision, and values to lead us to a new era in America. Dean has led a successful business, building Talenti Gelato into a national brand.

After Trump won, Dean felt he had to do more for his two daughters and the country. He ran for Congress and flipped a red-leaning district that hadn't been represented by a Democrat in over fifty years. No one thought he had a chance, but he ran a positive campaign with the slogan *Everyone's invited*. His last race he won by double digits and he's now in his third term. Dean has never lost a race.

I met Dean when he was in Congress two years ago at a campaign finance reform event, where he despaired that all of his colleagues spent thousands of hours a week dialing for dollars. He was the only member who didn't, figuring he was actually there to try to get things done. As you can imagine, I liked him immediately—imagine a member of Congress who doesn't like calling donors and is willing to say so.

Dean is running for president not because it somehow serves his interests, but because it is the right thing to do. He was alarmed that we were sleepwalking toward disaster and called other leading Democrats asking them to run. While people agreed with him in private, in public they toed the party line. They put their careers ahead of the country. Only when no one else stepped up did Dean take on the challenge himself. He thought of his father, who died in Vietnam in a helicopter crash serving our country. What would he do? Dean has now been accused of all sorts of things because that's the politics of today, but his decision to run for president is among the most courageous acts I have seen in American life. His father would be proud.

Dean is all in. You know one reason why members of Congress generally make terrible presidential candidates? It's because when the going gets tough, they often double back to seek reelection to their current seat. Not Dean. He gave up a safe congressional seat to try to save his country, giving up a promising career in party leadership out of duty. That is character, the kind of character that so many of our leaders today lack. If we had more people in Washington willing to upend their careers like Dean, we would be a much stronger country.

Dean has a compelling vision and motivation—to make America more affordable for working families. He knows that healthcare costs are the number one cause of bankruptcy in America—that's why he signed a Medicare for All bill that would finally ensure that all Americans have access to quality care. He wants to have a baby bond of $1,000 for every child born in America that would grow to be significant by the time that child is eighteen. He wants to bring back the enhanced child tax credit that lifted millions of American families out of poverty. He wants to ease our housing crisis by building seven million new housing units around the country. He wants to make college and vocational school alike cost-free so young people have a better shot at a brighter future.

These are the kind of goals that Americans of all parties and backgrounds can get excited about.

Dean will govern as a different type of president who puts leadership ahead of the letter next to your name. Dean will recruit the best people to his administration, from both within and outside of the party and government. It is impossible to reunite and repair our country while we are divided into two warring factions for the amusement of the media and the political industrial complex. Dean will literally repair America with the most nonpartisan, bipartisan cabinet anyone has ever seen.

Dean is not just for campaign finance reform but for open primaries, ranked-choice voting, and term limits. No one knows how dark the machinery is more than Dean. He may not seem like it because he's such a congenial guy, but Dean has the potential to be the most transformative leader we have seen in our lifetimes.

I ran for president and know that the people of this country are much better than the leadership we are getting, that we are united in much more than the parties and the partisan media would have you believe.

To those on the left who are progressive, Dean is our best chance to pass universal healthcare, get baby bonds, make housing more affordable, and alleviate meaningless suffering for millions of Americans.

To Democrats, Dean is our best chance to defeat Donald Trump once and for all and ensure that democracy persists and prevails. To Independents, Dean is our best chance to put the people's interests above the parties that separate and divide us and return government to the people. To moderate Republicans, Dean is the second most bipartisan member of Congress and will include you in the future as we move past Trump.

To journalists and influencers, wouldn't you rather cover a real primary process rather than slump into the battle of the eighty-year-olds? Dean's victory could be one of the greatest stories of this era.

To my friend Marianne Williamson, you have run a noble, courageous campaign and have articulated many of the things that Americans should expect and deserve. I ask you to join us in challenging the true enemy. The true enemy is the political establishment that does not care about our families and communities and a media cabal that will suppress or demonize those who want change on behalf of the people of this country. Marianne, Dean is our best chance to change things. I am looking forward to serving in his administration and I would love for you to join us.

For the voters of New Hampshire, I've

met thousands of you over the years and I know how seriously you take the trust of this country to pick a president. What does your heart tell you is the right thing to do? Are we going to career toward disaster, or will you save us and move the country forward in a new and better direction? Will we settle for politics as usual or will we try for something better? If you spend time with Dean, you will see that he has the makings of a tremendous president.

Dean is a sane, smart, pragmatic, fifty-four-year-old leader who wants to bring the country back together and improve our lives. He is unbeholden to the special interests who dominate our politics. He is the man for this moment. He is what most Americans—certainly most Independents, who will decide our elections—want in a candidate. Most of all, he will win.

What do you think, New Hampshire—do you want to help Dean win?

Me too. I'm proud to introduce the next president of the United States, Dean Phillips!

∽☙∾

Being Dean's hype man was a lot of fun—and a whole lot more chill than being the candidate. I would introduce him at rallies by saying, "Ladies and gentlemen, the next president of the United States, Dean Phillips!!!" and then go text with Evelyn while he was doing his thing. I felt a little bit like Zach.

It was a blast being up in my old presidential stomping grounds. I saw familiar faces and *MATH* hats. I spoke at my high school and saw parents of old friends. The energy was real. Dean got 19 percent of the primary vote, and it would have been much higher if the Independents hadn't all headed over to the Republican primary to vote for Nikki Haley against Donald Trump.

The press, however, were pretty determined to undermine or ignore Dean. The only photograph they showed from New Hampshire was him at an underattended daytime event in subzero weather the week before, not the crowds he was drawing down the stretch. And they acted like 19 percent wasn't substantial, when it was actually a historically high level against an incumbent.

Afterward, we went to South Carolina. Dean had no time and no money—we were a total nonfactor there. He got blown out, which more or less ended his campaign. When we were in South Carolina leading up to the vote, we attended a massive Democratic event. At one point, Dean leaned over to California governor Gavin Newsom and whispered in his ear, "You should have fucking run." Gavin responded with a fixed grin.

Joe Biden came to Columbia, South Carolina, to address the crowd and it was not great. He seemed old and wobbly, his skin translucent. Evelyn gasped when she saw him. Joe read his remarks off a teleprompter, haltingly. The crowd chanted, *"Four more years! Four more years!"* Evelyn and I looked at each other. "Four more *weeks* is more like it," I joked.

The scene was somehow dystopian, despite the fact that the South Carolina Democrats are warm, gracious, and lovely people. It affected Dean deeply.

You know the scarring I've talked about? Dean had a bit of that. And who could blame him? He did the right thing for his country by trying to force a primary that might have prevented Donald Trump's return. His reward? Being maligned as a narcissist, a premature end to his political career, and getting ostracized and shivved by his former friends and colleagues. When "no good deed goes unpunished" seems to be the law of the land, it can subvert your sense of well-being and goodwill.

Dean Phillips will always have my gratitude and admiration for demonstrating more character than all of the putative leaders who rushed to prop Joe up despite what we could all see. Others will forget, but the Yangs remember.

Joe Biden would drop out of the presidential race about five months later.

Chapter 36

Welcome to My TED Talk

"**C**an you do it in eleven minutes?"

"Sure," I responded. I could do a talk that ordinarily takes me about thirty minutes in eleven.

The person asking me was a delightful coach provided to me by TED. For those of you who don't know much about TED, it's a conference that convenes a host of thinkers in technology, science, and culture. The videos from people's talks are widely circulated—it has twenty-four million subscribers on YouTube, for example. A realistic expectation of the number of people who will wind up seeing your talk is probably one to three million, with a possibility of it being significantly higher—some talks reach more than ten million.

I had given a talk on America's primary elections at an event in New York a few months earlier. Afterward, a very smart-sounding British man came up to me. "That was brilliant. You should deliver that at TED this year." Turns out it was Chris Anderson, who runs TED.

I've spoken on America's political system dozens of times and feel very comfortable doing so. But having a tailored talk with slides on a tight time frame still required some thought and work. The TED team asks that you rehearse and present to them multiple times before the actual conference. My dress rehearsal on the actual stage was a little bit rocky, but that didn't bother me, as I often suck until it gets real. I'm a little bit like Allen Iverson: "Practice? We're talking about *practice*?" The venue holds about 1,700 people, and there's one "take." So there is definitely some pressure.

Evelyn flew out to join me for the occasion—she'd never attended TED before. I'd attended it the first time back in 2017 in the run-up to my presidential campaign. I'd figured I'd go and try to hustle up some supporters. Which didn't happen—I was more or less a guy in the crowd at that point—but I did have a great time. It's a very abundant environment with free stuff all over the place.

The night before my talk reminded me a little bit of a night before a presidential debate, where it's tough to get to sleep. I woke up thinking, *Today's the day!* I was eager to hit the message and was scheduled to speak at the morning session.

When I got to the green room, Scott Galloway was there preparing to speak before me, so we shared some tips and stories. Scott is a marketing professor at NYU known as "Prof G," though he's

199 ❖ Andrew Yang

a lot more than that. He's one of the most original thinkers in the country who actually has a point of view and a backbone. Scott gave a very compelling talk about how young people are screwed in the US today. It was fascinating because he had charts and figures on many of the trends I'd run on in 2020, and they had all gotten worse in the intervening four years.

Scott came off the stage to a rousing ovation. And then, after a very erudite introduction by Chris, I heard my name called and bounded to the stage.

"I'm speaking here in Canada," I began, "and a friend in Canada compared living here to living in the apartment above a meth lab; he's concerned about what's going on below him, and it's starting to concern the entire neighborhood." I broke down why America feels so divided, and how that schism is baked into the system. I then detailed a way we could change the voting system in a critical number of states for the low, low cost of $200 million and start bringing people back together. If this doesn't make any sense to you or you want more details, I invite you to watch my full TED Talk on YouTube right now. It will be the best 10.6 minutes you spend today!

I'm glad to say I got a standing ovation as well. People came up to me afterward to congratulate me. I definitely opened some eyes and minds to a different approach to the problems that ail us. One person said to me afterward, "Thank you. I feel like the future of civilization may rest on whether your efforts succeed." Others asked, "How can I help?" It felt awesome to deliver on what I knew was a big opportunity to get the word out.

Some people speak and then quietly slip out the back. I try to stick around, because people will often come up and want to help. In this case, it was very easy and natural to stay for the day because there were other interesting talks to attend.

I'm glad Evelyn was there to share in the experience. "Nice job!" she said to me. "You know whose talk is really going to go viral, though? Scott Galloway's. That topic is sexy. A whole lot sexier than yours."

We returned to New York and TED released our talks to the world a few weeks later. Mine, titled "Why US Politics Is Broken—and How to Fix It," has been viewed about 2.5 million times. I know it raised at least a million dollars for the open primary campaigns. It was the #7 TED Talk of 2024.

Meanwhile, Scott Galloway's speech, "How the US Is Destroying Young People's Futures," has been viewed 14.8 million times and was the #1 TED Talk of the year. As usual, Evelyn was right.

Chapter 37
Pass the Torch

"**E**ighty-one-year-old man holds nation hostage—film at eleven."

On June 27, 2024, Joe Biden and Donald Trump debated. It was a fiasco. Biden was so inarticulate and lethargic that Trump almost seemed to feel bad for him. I watched it shaking my head, then posted the following on social media:

Guys, the Dems should nominate someone else—before it's too late. #swapJoeout

Look, I debated Joe 7 times in 2020. He's a different guy in 2024. #swapJoeout

My phone blew up. *#swapJoeout* started trending as my posts got millions of views, comments, and reposts. I hadn't expected to hit such a nerve. Reporters from the *Washington Post*, ABC, Yahoo, and the *Wall Street Journal* called and texted me asking for more. "Are you willing to say something on the record about Joe stepping aside?"

"Sure," I responded. At this point I was already on blast, so I might as well lean into it. It boggled my mind how the Dems were to that point content to run Joe toward what appeared to be a certain loss. Plus, one of the joys of being a Forward Independent is that you can support a good Democrat, Republican, or Independent candidate as you see fit. It's not about a particular party but the best person and outcome in a particular race, along with reforming the system so more people can vote how they choose.

I spent the next several weeks bashing Joe Biden's decision to keep running. I told Evelyn that every morning I asked myself, *How can I best undermine our president today?* I became a regular on cable news, making the case that Joe was a weak, flawed, aging, unpopular nominee, and that the Democrats would be much better off moving on from him. I connected journalists with donors who had soured on Joe to fuel negative stories. I also supported a new political action committee— PasstheTorch.com—that was raising money for advertisements and activities trying to get Joe to do the right thing. This endeavor culminated in a protest in front of the White House with people holding signs begging Joe to *Pass the Torch* for all of our sakes.

Watching various Democrats come out and

vouch for Joe's faculties was surreal. I'd seen the guy in person five months earlier and he had looked like he'd just stepped out of a wax museum. At one point he brought a bunch of governors to the White House and had them do a press conference for him; it looked like a hostage video as some governors slipped out the back.

I spoke to folks in DC every day during this time. The energy rose and fell. Some days people were ready to give up hope. If there's one person who fanned the flames the most, it was probably Nancy Pelosi, who would comment, "We're still waiting for Joe to make up his mind," every time Joe would say, "I'm running!" Ultimately, Chuck Schumer, Hakeem Jeffries, and Pelosi went to Joe in Delaware and told him that he needed to pull out. Barack Obama was already urging the same without being public about it.

Joe finally dropped out on July 27. There was a brief period when everyone was like, "Will there by a primary?" "Is it Kamala?" Then, only two hours after dropping out, Joe endorsed Kamala.

My entire network was ablaze for about eighteen hours, asking, "Is anyone going to run against Kamala for the nomination?"

During this time, I was prodding people for a competitive primary. I joked to my team that we should change the name of the Pass the Torch PAC to Keep Passing the Torch or Pass the Torch Again. I had run against Kamala in 2020, which meant I had spoken at town halls and forums before and after her, interacted with her off camera many times, and been on a debate stage with her five times.

In my opinion, she had a couple of fundamental problems as a candidate. The first is that, when asked a question, she seemed to be thinking, *What should I say here?* instead of, *What do I think?* or, *What do I believe?* This made her responses seem hesitant and inauthentic. She was, simply put, an unconvincing interview. That's a real challenge on a presidential campaign.

The second problem was that four years earlier, she didn't have a clear message or vision for her campaign and why *she* should be president, and I wasn't sure that was going to change. I remembered at one event in Iowa, she swept in on a big campaign bus and spoke to a group of activists. She was the main draw; I was kind of the afterthought. She gave twelve minutes of remarks about Trump and America, took some pictures, and left. I distinctly recall saying to myself, *I don't think she won over anyone in this room*, in part because her reasons for running were fuzzy at best. She wound up dropping out a few weeks later, before the voting started.

Her underperformance in 2020 as well as her being tied to an unpopular administration convinced me that she was not the best choice to replace Joe. I thought the best choice would

205 ♣ Andrew Yang

have been a governor of a swing state—Josh Shapiro (Pennsylvania) or Gretchen Whitmer (Michigan)—who could distance him- or herself from the problems of the administration. "Pissed off at the border? Me too! I had nothing to do with it, I was in Harrisburg. Let's fix it!"

I believed that Joe Biden would lead to a historic loss, and Kamala Harris to a dignified loss, while a Whitmer-Shapiro ticket would be competitive and maybe even win. That ticket probably got you two of the three swing states you needed from the get-go and then you could fight it out in Wisconsin with everything you had. That was, at least, an approach with a chance of success.

This was all going down in the hours after Joe's endorsement of Kamala. People were calling all of the usual suspects. The main two figures who were known to have campaigns-in-waiting were Gavin Newsom and JB Pritzker. Kamala was working the phones on every delegate. More and more Democrats were coming out saying, "Kamala it is! She's the greatest!"

One by one, every contender came out and endorsed Kamala, just about hourly. Andy Beshear. Gavin Newsom. Josh Shapiro. Gretchen Whitmer. When JB Pritzker endorsed her, everyone I knew gave up. He was the only one left. "Well, it's over, we tried."

Eventually, even Barack Obama and Nancy Pelosi, who had clearly been in favor of a primary, capitulated, and the anointment of Kamala Harris was complete. Democracy triumphed by preventing an actual contest.

Why did Joe endorse Kamala? I think a lot of it was that he was pushed to do so by Congressman Jim Clyburn, to whom he arguably owed his presidency. I also think that if she'd won, it would have been good for Joe's legacy. "Not only did I defeat Trump, but then I got the first black woman elected president." And then if she lost, he could say, "See, it should have been *me* all along." The folks around Joe likely thought that they'd have a much better chance at keeping their jobs on the campaign if Kamala took over, as her name was already on the ticket. Last, I think it was kind of a "fuck you" to Pelosi and Obama for ousting him.

One thing that I don't believe was that Joe thought that Kamala was a very strong candidate. He had essentially been saying to people just weeks prior, "I need to be the nominee, because if not me, who? Kamala?" That's not exactly a ringing vote of confidence.

Still, despite all of my misgivings, I accepted reality. I had been fighting for months for the Democratic Party to move on from Joe Biden and have a real primary. They had done one but not the other. Kamala Harris was going to be the nominee. It would be her or Trump. The next day, I posted an endorsement message for Kamala accompanied by a picture of the two of us in Iowa four years earlier. I knew I was never going to support Trump. Heck, trying to fix the problems that got Trump elected was what got me into public life in the first place, and to me he's the answer like junk food is the answer to kidney disease.

Chapter 38

Election Day

On election night, it obviously didn't go well for Kamala Harris and the Dems, as they lost all seven swing states and vote share in just about every county. The Age of Trump was back.

I spent that night in Philadelphia with a lot of the Forward Party leaders and activists, including local candidates. I did press from the parking lot outside, which made for an interesting backdrop. There were a couple of emotionally unstable homeless guys circulating.

Elon Musk, who had endorsed me four years earlier, had been giving away one million dollars a day in Pennsylvania to voters who signed a petition. I joked, "You know how Elon endorsed me in the last election? If he had given away one million dollars a day in Iowa in 2020, I might be president today."

Kamala Harris's campaign had put me on a list of people to *not* use or refer to, due to the fact that I'd "crossed the line" in my disrespect of Joe

Biden during Dean Phillips's campaign and the Pass the Torch activities. So dumb. I was kind of glad, to be honest, because if they'd asked me to do something, I would have felt honor bound to comply, but I don't know how convincing I would have been. Evelyn said that my endorsement of Kamala in *Newsweek* was one of the most tepid things she had ever read. Still, this approach was a sign of a culture problem—if you're trying your best to win, who cares what I said four weeks ago? Use anyone who might move votes.

The result—Trump winning—didn't surprise me. It had been what I thought was the most probable outcome since earlier in the year. Perhaps the most glaring mistake of the Kamala Harris campaign was deciding not to do an interview with Joe Rogan. It would have reached tens of millions of men, many of them low-proclivity voters. It's the biggest audience in media, rivaling the number of people who watched the presidential debates. If Harris and Tim Walz had been more effective in their interviews, maybe Joe Rogan would have decided to stay neutral instead of endorsing Trump. At the time, I was totally mystified. I thought, *Maybe they know something I don't. Like they're secretly ahead by five points?* The only other explanation was that they didn't want to run the risk of Kamala saying something really embarrassing.

By the way, the explanation offered by the campaign was that they just couldn't make it work with their schedule. This is total nonsense. I was a candidate; what happens is your campaign manager says to you, "Okay, there's a Joe Rogan interview possibility. This is a much bigger deal than the events and fundraisers we have on tap, so we'll move *this* around, cancel *this*, and get you to Austin next week. Cool?" You say, "Great," and it happens. Which is exactly what transpired when Kamala decided to do *Saturday Night Live* the weekend before the debate or any of a ton of other interviews. You know what's going to move the needle and your campaign prioritizes accordingly.

A rumor spread that some of the more radical junior staffers were upset at the idea of their candidate sitting with Joe Rogan. This also didn't make any sense given that it was unlikely the junior staffers' opinions would determine candidate scheduling, and besides, Kamala had already sat for interviews on Fox News with Bret Baier and the like.

Some speculated that Rogan didn't want to have Kamala on his show, which doesn't seem credible. Rogan publicly said he'd love to have her on. He had John Fetterman on, and who wouldn't want to host both major candidates if you're a media figure?

What most likely happened was that someone in Kamala's campaign looked at the Joe Rogan possibility and said, "This is more risk than reward," or, "We don't trust our candidate to sit there and have a two- or three-hour conversation without a gaffe or doing something very regrettable." Basically, someone was probably more worried about fucking up than giving themselves the best chance to win. The shame of it is that I think Rogan would have been courteous and curious, and not some interrogator with an agenda. "My sincere wish is to just have a nice conversation and get to know her as a human being" is how he described it.

In the days afterward, some pundits wrote that America would never elect a woman of color as president. My first thought was, *I don't know, maybe run one who is good at doing interviews so we can find out.* In any case, the biggest media audience in the country got ceded to Trump without any real contest, contributing to his clean sweep in the swing states.

I did a lot of press in the days afterward. When they asked me, "Why did Kamala Harris lose to Trump?" I said, "The Democrats' big problem was that they didn't have a primary back in January when it could have made a difference. They actually tied with Republicans among voters who cited 'democracy' as their main issue. It's hard to say that you're defending democracy when you didn't have a primary yourself. It's also the case that whoever emerged from a primary would have been vetted and among your best candidates."

Imagine what a Democratic primary would have looked like: Andy Beshear, Gretchen Whitmer,

Josh Shapiro, Gavin Newsom, Wes Moore, JB Pritzker, and a host of other candidates making their case. Millions of Americans tuning in, getting to know a new generation. Dean Phillips gave his political career to try to make that happen.

Speaking of which, the Democratic Party's entire identity is going to be up for grabs until they settle on a nominee in 2028. Here's who I think will run: everyone. Newsom, Pritzker, Shapiro, Moore, Whitmer, and Beshear, along with Jared Polis, Ro Khanna, Amy Klobuchar, Pete Buttigieg, AOC, Tim Walz, Raphael Warnock, Chris Murphy, Cory Booker, Ruben Gallego, Rahm Emanuel, and another dozen or so who look at the field and think, *Hey, I might as well.* There will be at least one businessperson who's a nonpolitician.

Would I run for president in '28? More on this later.

Chapter 39

How to Make All Americans Totally Happy

I've figured out how we can make all Americans feel great about how things are going after the next election. Bear with me.

Derek Thompson is one of my favorite journalists; he writes about economics and technology and has a podcast on the Ringer called *Plain English*. Awhile back, I asked him a simple question: "What is going on with the economy?"

He said something that blew my mind: "Well, there's what's *actually* going on in the economy. And then there's what people *feel*. It turns out that the way you feel about the economy primarily relies upon how you feel about whoever's in the White House."

Derek cited the Michigan consumer confidence survey at the time. That month, when Joe Biden was still president, there was an enormous difference between how Republicans and Democrats felt things were going. Republicans had it at a 37.8 on a 140-point scale—which is terrible. Democrats had it at 88.4—not too bad. Independents were in between at 70. This 49-point gap was the biggest in the history of the survey, which spans almost eighty years. Democrats were fine with the economy, Republicans were unhappy.

Okay, you're thinking, *maybe Democrats were more optimistic or living in areas with better economic conditions?* But the gap went the other direction during Trump's first term. Back then, Republicans were at 119, Democrats at 71.6, and Independents at 100, for a swing of 47 points. That was the second biggest gap in history.

Derek went on to say, "Instead of asking you about the economy, I could ask you how you feel about the president, and then I'd know how you feel about the economy."

That's crazy. But it also gives us the answer to how we can make all Americans think things are going great all of the time: give the next loser of the presidential election a four-year TV contract to live in a replica of the White House! You want to see your president? Just tune in to your favorite cable network. They'll be there signing things, saying things you enjoy, holding court. Acting presidential.

Think about it—what better way to avoid civil war at a time when 42 percent of both Republicans and Democrats think the other side is "evil" or their "mortal enemies"? Let them think they won.

The fact is, whoever wins the next election, the other side is going to feel terrible. Why not have *both* win? This way, everyone gets what they want. One person becomes president. The other gets a four-year TV contract with lodging and servants and fake Secret Service. They could get paid the same $400k salary as the president. You're welcome, America.

Two presidents: because Americans can't handle disappointment.

The journalist Michael Grunwald wrote in *POLITICO*: "There is a line of thinking that America has entered a kind of postmodern political era where the appearance of governing is just as politically powerful as actual governing, because most Americans now live in partisan spin bubbles that insulate them from the facts on the ground."

He's right. Let's lean into it. Let's give everyone the bubble they want. According to Derek, the facts on the ground aren't that relevant anyway.

Now, I know what you're thinking: *Why stop at two?* If you're reading this, you might be among the group of Americans who wanted *me* to be president. Why not make a third president? I think I could talk Evelyn into hanging out in a fake White House as long as the food was real. And the people watching our channel should get $1,000 a month—after all, we have to make it realistic. I choose . . . ESPN. Put our replica White House someplace really sunny.

Let's Make Americans Totally Happy—the new MATH—all of the time.

What do you think?

Or, if the above isn't plausible, we could . . . get our acts together.

If we can't have multiple fake presidents, my plan is to make the case far and wide that we're still actually a pretty awesome land filled with lovely, wonderful people. Sure, we have our differences, but we have so much more that brings us together. For example, we all harbor contempt for other countries. What are you going to do, move to Canada? *Bo-ring.*

America: love it or leave it. I'm not going anywhere. Neither are you. Stop pretending. Let's get to work.

Part VI

THE FUTURE

Chapter 40
The Economy of the Future

In late April of '24, I hosted the first ever Hudson Valley Ideas Fest.

What the heck is that? I had spoken in Aspen at their Ideas Fest the year before. The mountains reminded me of the Hudson Valley, where my family spends a lot of time, and I thought, *We should do that here!* I figured it would be a good time for speakers and residents alike.

I called up a bunch of my friends and invited them to talk at a local community theater. The public speakers were Stephen Dubner (*Freakonomics*), Xochitl Gonzalez (the *Atlantic*), Coleman Hughes (CNN and the *Free Press*), Rikki Schlott (*New York Post*), and Stephen Marche (novelist and essayist). A couple hundred people showed up, which was a nice crowd.

At dinner afterward, I got to talking to Stephen Dubner. Stephen is a storytelling genius and the podcast he produces, *Freakonomics Radio*, gets about 2.5 million listeners a week. He said to me,

"Hey, I've been reading this book *No More Throw-Away People* and have been getting very interested in the idea of 'timebanking.' Do you want to work on it with me?"

"Heck yes! Love that book!" I responded.

What was this book he was talking about and what is timebanking? Edgar Cahn had been a speechwriter for Bobby Kennedy and later became deeply concerned about the automation of jobs—sound familiar? He wrote a book in 2000 that called for a new economy—timebanking—in which people barter time to help others in their community. For example, if I babysit your child, I could earn an hour of time, which I could then give to someone else to shovel my driveway, who could then use it to get someone else to cook them a meal. The theory is that just about everyone can make a contribution—we're just not giving people the right connections and opportunities.

I had advocated for a similar system using a new currency—digital social credits—in *The War on Normal People*. During the presidential campaign, Zach made me swear never to talk about it. Quoth Zach, "It's hard enough to get people on board with the Asian tech guy who wants to give everyone free money, but if you start talking about new currencies or timebanking, people's brains shut off. Plus, the social credit thing makes people think of China where they rate everyone. No one's voting for *Black Mirror*."

Still, Stephen and I had independently arrived at the conclusion that this could help revitalize communities in an era when AI was going to show up and eat our jobs. AI is now doubling in speed and scope every seven months—the last time humans double in brain capacity in such a short time is in the first year of life. Middle-aged guys like me are happy just to not get dumber in a given week. We are going to have to fuel a different kind of economy if we want people to thrive. Imagine an economy based on arts and creativity, or health and wellness, or caring and nurturing, in addition to capital efficiency. That's where we need to go.

Basically, if the economy is only based on doing work quickly and cheaply, humans are going to lose on a colossal scale to technology. So the only smart thing to do is change the terms of the race so that we get to do things that we both *want* to do and that will produce what we need more of. How is it that we have so many problems that could be solved by other humans, including a loneliness crisis, while people are just lying around at home?

Our economy might have worked for a long time. But now AI is going to break it, and we need a redesign.

Stephen hosted me on his podcast later that year for an episode called "The World's Most Valuable Unused Resource." That refers to our time, which isn't being used to help each other, and there's an awful lot of it. At the end of the episode, we asked people to get in touch if they wanted to help make timebanking a reality.

We got hundreds of applicants and thousands of messages from around the world. A lot of incredible people were into this concept. Several weeks later, we identified Jenny Kassan, an attorney from the Bay Area with a passion for building communities. She had already begun investing in Baltimore to try to support local activists and businesses. "I've wanted to make timebanking happen for years, particularly hand in hand with other forms of investment." We established a pilot program called Baltimore Community Commons and are presently fundraising for it.

Can we establish the economy of the future that revolves around humanity? It's early days, but we certainly have to try. A very smart guy named R. Buckminster Fuller wrote, "Whether it is to be Utopia or Oblivion will be a touch-and-go relay race right up to the final moment." He's likely right, and we need to give Utopia a real running start.

Yes, I am trying to create a new type of economy. And you must help me. Send me your Social Security number right now. Kidding! At least about that last part.

You know what's not Utopia? The US circa 2026, the slogan of which should probably be, *Designed to extract maximum profit from as many of us as possible*. We really could do a whole lot better.

Chapter 41

Gone in Sixty Seconds

"Hey, are you running again?"

I get a version of this question just about every day. It's touching.

My standard response is, "Apparently, I've got thirty more years."

That almost always gets a laugh. And then a response like, "I'm not sure we have that much time."

Of course I think about it. I joke to Evelyn, "You do realize that I'm always only sixty seconds away from running for president."

What do I mean? If I were to take my smartphone and post a sixty-second video saying, "In 2020, I ran for president to solve the biggest problems of our time, including poverty in the face of AI. Since then, the problems have only grown worse, and solutions are harder to come by. Americans deserve better. We will end poverty in our time. I am proud to announce that I will be running for president in 2028! Go to andrewyang.

com to learn more. Thank you, YangGang—we are back and it's time to finish the job!"

If I were to post that video, even a janky one, to my social media platforms, just about every major news outlet in the country would run a piece, or at least mention, "Andrew Yang Announces Run for President in '28." It would get millions of views. I would get hundreds or thousands of messages asking, "How can I help?" and myriad texts saying, *I can't believe you didn't let me know before announcing!* Major press outlets would reach out asking to have me on or for an interview, along with a significant number of podcasters and influencers. I would need a day or so to set up a donation link and a campaign account, but we would be off to the races pretty quickly. This is true for me in a way that is probably true for a few dozen other people in the country; it's newsworthy for me to run in a way it wouldn't be for even the average member of Congress or some senators.

Don't believe me? Here's a test: let's say that a US senator decided to run for president. Can you pick out which of these five people is a current US senator? Jim Banks, Kevin Cramer, Deb Fischer, Roger Marshall, John Boozman.

It's a trick question—all of them are!

Let's try again: which of these five people is a US senator? John Barrasso, Ted Budd, Ashley Moody, Jerry Moran, Dan Sullivan.

Also all of them! If one of them decided to run

for president, the average American would be like
. . . *Who?* I could have totally made names up just
now. As a matter of fact, here goes: John Hoeven,
Jon Husted, Cindy Hyde-Smith, Jim Risch, Roger
Wicker.

Those were senators again! I could do this all
day.

It bears mentioning that I'm also always sixty
seconds away from ending my public-facing career as well; all it would take is a video saying, "I,
Andrew Yang, love putting gerbils in my pants,
like that Richard Gere story from the eighties but
in real life. That's actually what gave me the idea.
It's great! You have to try it. I have kept it to myself
for so long, but that is my reality. It feels so good
to share this with you. Humanity First"—or some
such, and that would be that. Permanent retire-
ment from public life, always within my grasp!

Jokes aside, the odds of my running again are
high. I like people. I love the country and those
within it. And I have some ideas for how to campaign better next time. For example, imagine if we
could vote on our smartphone in a primary that
included everyone, including Independents?

Let's just say that I'm constantly evaluating,
and there are different ways to make good things
happen. I have an uncommon privilege of being
sixty seconds away, sort of like actor Nicolas Cage,
who donated to my presidential campaign. How
did I not win?

Chapter 42

Twenty-Three Weddings

S omeone told me that there's a Jewish notion that if you introduce two people who end up getting married, you make it into heaven.

Well, I'm sort-of-kind-of responsible for twenty-two weddings that I know of, not including my own. I was the CEO of Manhattan Prep for five years, and eight of my colleagues there married coworkers. There were a lot of young, eligible people working at that company and we were a festive bunch.

Now, you might say, "Sure, you were the CEO of the company, but could you really take credit for people getting married?" Good point. However, in 2011 I started Venture for America, a fellowship program for aspiring entrepreneurs to work for two years at start-ups in cities like Detroit, New Orleans, Birmingham, and Baltimore. Young, thirsty college graduates would show up for VFA, work among each other in various cities for two years, and then often stick around.

227 ❖ Andrew Yang

They had social events up the wazoo, including Philly Phormal, a giant nightclub party. You can imagine the relationships that ensued. At last count, someone told me that there were eighteen VFAer-married-another-VFAer couples that have formed over the years.

Eighteen! And you'd have to say I played a pretty big role in those by starting the org. I got invited to a lot of those weddings. That number will likely go up over time too.

I know a few people who met on my campaign and started dating, so it's only a matter of time before I get to Wedding #23. One couple got married but then got divorced, so it doesn't count.

Am I done hooking people up? Not a chance. I'm going for at least thirty before I give up. There are a lot of single people out there. If you're looking for love, come find me. I'm going to Cupid everyone before I'm through. What kind of person are you looking for?

Chapter 43

Asian Superguy

In April 2024, I opened up for Dave Chappelle in his comedy club in Yellow Springs, Ohio, a converted firehouse that he bought and turned into a venue. Dave had invited me there to check it out. He joked, "I spend my money buying up old buildings in this town and making them nice. If I were white, you'd call it gentrification. But because I'm black . . . there's no word for what I'm doing."

Dave introduced me by saying, "Here's the guy who got everything right in 2020, but no one listened because he's Asian—Andrew Yang!"

I came out and began, "Hey, everyone, how are you doing? Yes, I did run for president. Any of you support me?"

Crickets.

"Well, fuck you then. Fuck you all."

Laughter.

I go on: "The magical Asian man from the future comes and wants to give you all money. And you're like, *I don't know . . . let me wait and see* *if someone else comes with a better offer. Maybe $2,000?"*

I had a tight five minutes on a variety of topics, including: filming videos with Dave and me saying "I'm Chris Tucker . . ." ". . . and I'm Jackie Chan. It's *Rush Hour* again, America!"; how Minions are racist; traveling in Asia with my kids and losing one of them at the mall; the two old guys then running for president; Asian male stereotypes; and how social media is killing us and how people getting together at a comedy club to have a few laughs is the antidote. I then shared a few kind words about Dave and closed with an "O-H?"

"I-O!" the crowd responded. It's an easy way to wrap a speech in Ohio, and also works for a quick comedy bit.

A lot of my routine was about being Asian. During one of the presidential debates, I had joked, "I'm Asian, so I know a lot of doctors," to a health-care question. I took a little bit of shit for that. Some said I was playing into Asian stereotypes.

You know what doesn't reinforce *any* Asian stereotype? Running for president.

After the campaign, I was in Alabama for a charity event one evening. A Southern gentleman in a business suit approached and extended his hand to me. "Mr. Yang, I don't agree with you on a whole lot, sir, but you've got a set of balls on you, and I respect that a great deal."

I put my hand on his shoulder and said, "Thank you. Just doing what I can for the country."

I get a similar reaction from all sorts of people. I was at a nightclub several years ago and a group of Asian guys freaked out when they saw me. One of them put his arm around me and started exclaiming to his friends, "See this guy? This guy fucks! He definitely fucks!!!" They offered to buy me drinks all night. I took a couple pictures and high-fived them before splitting.

I once read a book about Asian Americans by Jay Caspian Kang called *The Loneliest Americans*. One of the main ideas is that no one cares about Asian American identity, and the author describes the tension of writing a book that argues no one cares about the subject. It made me laugh, but it also felt familiar.

There's a stereotype of an "Angry Asian Man" who goes to the gym, listens to hip-hop, and feels alienated, cursing to himself as he curls weights. I certainly resembled that in my twenties, before I met Evelyn. Have I been mistaken for a delivery guy by a Manhattan doorman because I was carrying a plastic bag? Sure. Some teenagers yelled "Ching chong!" at me from a car window in New England a few years back, and I found myself more confused and saddened by it than anything else.

I sometimes tell my boys to work hard, which can include basic things like helping with the groceries or luggage. Occasionally, I'll say something kind of harsh, like, "This country has no use for a lazy Asian guy." We're sort of here to work. I remember trying to fit in when I was growing up, which was its own form of work.

I try to recall those times of fierce insecurity and questioning whether I would find my place in the world, feeling pain and alienation that were so deeply a part of me. But it's harder and harder to recollect that version of me; I'm now the Asian Superguy. Weakness has no utility and will be seized on. I walk into a TV studio or conference or club and the curtains part. Nearly everyone likes having someone famous around.

Let's talk about the future.

Chapter 44

Those Who Have Passed

Mike Skinner, one of my partners throwing parties years ago, died prematurely of a heart attack as he was about to turn forty. That was tough on everyone who knew him, as he was incredibly full of life. We had some great times.

A number of people died more recently whom I miss dearly. My friend Don Sun died of cancer in the spring of 2024. If you were on the campaign, you knew Don. He was with us every step of the way, folding his legs so he could fit in the rental vehicle, always smiling. I still miss him—he believed in me more than perhaps anyone else. On his deathbed, he said to me, "You are the one who can bring us together."

Norm Macdonald said that I was ahead of my time and helped the campaign before passing away from cancer. Bob Saget, whose wife told me that he loved me, died while on tour. Trevor Pierce, a college student from New Hampshire who was a huge supporter, died in a skateboarding accident on campus. I consoled Trevor's mom, who told me, "He really believed in you."

It has felt like the #YangGang has lost a lot of people in the past several years. Wanito, the military veteran who tattooed a Yang emoji on his calf; he had substance abuse problems. Brutum, another military vet, one who suffered from PTSD, passed last year. Elizabeth Norris. Ewoks4UBI. Kyle Christensen's mom in Iowa lost her battle with cancer. H.P. Wang in Schenectady, who treated me like a long-lost son, also died of cancer.

I suppose if you have a movement of thousands of supporters and add five years, things will happen to a host of people. Good things happen too—people having kids and getting married and falling in love, maybe not in that order.

Back in 2020 I had a morbid thought—what would it look like if I were to pass away? What would happen at the ceremony? Some people are frozen in time for us because they died at a particular moment. But I put that thought out of my head. I've got a ton in front of me and a lot of people relying on me, starting with a couple little guys.

It's like Andy Dufresne says in *The Shawshank Redemption*: "Get busy living or get busy dying." We don't have unlimited time on this world. Those who pass remind us to make the most of it.

Chapter 45
Social Media

A friend recently said to me over dinner, "Hey, I quit using Instagram. Thank you."

I didn't understand. Had something happened with me on Instagram? "Why?"

"I've been posting pictures for months," he explained, "and chatting with people and trying to gain followers." He's a doctor. "After doing this for more than a year, I finally got up to five thousand followers. And I felt happy. But then I looked at your account and realized you have hundreds of thousands of followers. I'll never get there. So I thought, *What's the point?* I quit a couple weeks ago and now I'm happier. I don't think, *Oh, I should take a picture of that*, when I see something that people might like anymore. I'm more relaxed. So thanks."

"Don't mention it," I said, since I'd literally done nothing.

Social media is not great. It likely makes us unhappier. But I currently have between two and three million followers across X, Instagram, and TikTok, and am working on building the path to Utopia. So I'd better do something with each platform.

I know hundreds of people whom I have never met in person. Occasionally, I meet someone with whom I've been digitally connected for years and we're like, "Finally!!!" I'm constantly getting some version of, "Huh, you're _____ in person than I thought you were." The two words I get most often are "taller" and "nicer." I guess I seem shorter and meaner online?

In 2023, the app formerly known as Twitter started to pay me a little bit—about $150 a month. It felt weird to be getting paid to do something I had been doing for free. So I decided to give it to my followers at random. After all, if they weren't following me, I wouldn't be getting paid. And I didn't want to feel beholden to the app for money. I also hoped maybe some other famous accounts would follow suit.

During the "Pass the Torch, Joe" era, my account was particularly highly trafficked on X and I got paid $432 for a two-week period. I hesitated. Should I give that away? It was more than I'd anticipated. And I laughed thinking, *Wow, my integrity can be bought for a few hundred bucks!* I went ahead and gave it away.

Then, around Election Day, the app paid me $1,900. That was a *lot*! Too much to give away to a total stranger? What was my price? I felt like the app was testing me. It got up to $2,292. I could keep it. No one would ever know.

Nah, not my style. You've got to let the energy flow. To date, I've given $16,500+ away on X. It's a good reason to keep using it, even though the platform has gotten a lot more negative and obnoxious.

A couple months ago, I had a Zoom with the leaders of Bluesky. They were impressive and I believe genuine in their desire to build a better social media experience. I resolved to spend more time on Bluesky.

A lot of the reason that America is so ticked off is that we've been reduced to having conversations with digital avatars instead of actual humans. I spent years on the road having face-to-face conversations with people from all walks of life, from truck stops in Iowa to inner-city Brooklyn. Just about everyone is open, cordial, and courteous if you are there in real life, particularly if you have come to them where they live.

I was in a long-distance relationship back in college. Stress built up because a phrase in an email came across as a little curt and was open to interpretation. It seemed that almost anything we emailed to each other would get skewed toward the negative. Our insecurities would emerge. We would get into fights about the dumbest things imaginable. *Why did you say that? Why* didn't *you say that? Why did you use that word?*

Does that remind you of anything? It reminds me of America on social media. America is in a long-distance relationship with itself. I swore off long-distance relationships after college as a result of that experience. Who knew that they would come to define our country. Social media in general is driving us into online corners where we engage in clashes, some of which drive behavior in real life. I have met people who seem like lunatics online and they're a hundred times better and more reasonable-seeming in person. I am wholly on board with social psychologist and author Jonathan Haidt's "anxious generation" message that we should restrict social media use for minors. I live in fear of my kids getting on social media when they're a few years older. I periodically go for nature walks to try to detox, often from something online.

In early 2025, I read an article in the *Atlantic* that explored how people don't party as much as they used to. That made me sad. I thought, *Hey, I could probably throw a good party if I put my mind to it*. I was, after all, a veteran party promoter. One of my former staffers, Conrad Taylor, had become a successful DJ. He agreed to perform. We booked a lounge downtown and threw an "Offline" no-phones party. We promoted it on Instagram and TikTok—finally, a good use for my social media accounts!

Three hundred and fifty people showed up.

When they arrived, we put everyone's phone in a little pouch that they got to keep with them. We put twenty-dollar bills in some of the pouches just for fun. Everyone had a blast. "I actually met some new people," a friend told me, "in part because none of us had a phone to look at."

It was such a success that we did it again the following month in an uptown club. This time seven hundred people showed up! By the time you read this, thousands of people will have gone to an Offline Party, as we decided to make it a series in cities around the country. You can find out more at offlineparty.com.

There's a real hunger for community and activity that translates out into the real world. Social media is supposed to make meeting people easier, not replace them.

Chapter 46
Turning Fifty

When I was a kid, I did not like my birthdays at all. I didn't have many friends—as I've mentioned, I was shy and bookish—so any celebration was hard to pull off. My mom would try to do something for my birthday, like bring me a cake or a rented movie from Blockbuster, but it always felt like our little celebration fell short. I definitely appreciate my mom for trying.

In part because of my childhood memories, as an adult I've tried to have fun on my birthdays. When I turned thirty, I got people together at a bar in New York. When I turned forty, we had a vacation in Puerto Rico, where Evelyn and I had gotten married, and invited friends and family to come celebrate.

When I turned forty-five, I was on the campaign trail so hundreds of people sang me "Happy Birthday" in Iowa with a giant cake. That was essentially the opposite of the modest, kind of pathetic celebrations that had been more the norm for me growing up.

So what to do for my big 5-0? The choice in my mind was simple: either be morose about it or have the biggest party possible.

I resolved to go as big as I could. I sent out a save-the-date notice months in advance. I decided to book a club in New York City for dinner and then have an after-party. I called friends who could DJ or sing or perform up-close magic and asked them if they would be the entertainment to make the night special.

Evelyn asked, "How many people are you going to invite?" Keep in mind that I have a lot of people I feel indebted to for believing in me over the last handful of years. I replied, "Geez, I don't know, hundreds." I knew that many of the people I'd invite wouldn't be able to make it, as they lived across the country or abroad and had families. But your fiftieth birthday is one of the last good reasons you have to ask people to travel and come see you. Think about it—what happens afterward? Turning *sixty*?

At some point Evelyn said, "If this is going to happen right, I need to be the one handling it." She was right, of course. She joked, "It's like a wedding, only you're renewing your vows . . . to yourself." After Evelyn took over, everything went up a notch.

In total, about six hundred and fifty people came to help me ring in my birthday on January 11, 2025. My brother reminisced about our childhood. Zach took out a scroll that unfurled to list "Things that Andrew Yang doesn't care about," with #1 being "His appearance." Evelyn gave a funny and heartfelt speech. Dave Chappelle talked about joining me on the trail and told some jokes—having the greatest comedian of all time commemorate my half century on the planet was a huge honor.

The celebration went late into the night. It was great seeing friends from different periods of my life catching up after not seeing each other for years. Evelyn and I helped shut the place down, getting pizza at three in the morning in true New York fashion. My kids got to participate in the early part of the evening. My twelve-year-old commented the next day, "You have a lot of friends, Dad." It's true.

It was an awesome night. I heartily recommend going big if you can for any life celebrations. Afterward I said to Evelyn, "That was so much fun, I want to do it again in much less than ten years." I'm planning to give us a reason to celebrate.

Chapter 47

The Canon

I mentioned before that I've written three non-fiction books, two of which were bestsellers. Chances are you haven't read all of them. I am now going to summarize 723 pages of nonfiction prose for you in one hundred words or less:

Smart People Should Build Things (2014): "Hey, our smart folks should do dope stuff like start companies in Detroit or New Orleans and not just head to Wall Street or Big Tech."

The War on Normal People (2018): "AI is going to come and eat our jobs, so we should start giving people money and do the economy differently in a way that we dig."

Forward (2021): "The two-party system isn't going to solve our problems, so we should try to get beyond it. We're going to need a third party and ranked-choice voting."

I did it in eighty-two words! Did I just discourage people from reading everything I've ever written? Here are a couple bonus books:

Longshot by Zach Graumann (2022): "Yang was a puppet, a front. It was all me, Zach Graumann."

The Last Election, a novel cowritten with Stephen Marche (2023): "Shit is going to get weirder than you think faster than you think."

Despite my prolific writings, including a weekly newsletter at andrewyang.com, I consider myself a doer and builder first and foremost. I am still trying to make the human-centered economy happen.

If you're someone who wants to see the vision come to pass, do check out Humanity Forward (wholesome advocacy in DC) and/or the Forward Party (creating a political alternative). I promise there are incredible people there.

With this book you are holding, the canon has grown. How best to summarize?

Hey Yang, Where's My Thousand Bucks? (2026): "Sometimes the truth is stranger—and funnier—than fiction." Or, "Keep trying. You never know what's going to hit."

Chapter 48

"How do you keep going?"

"How do you keep going?" I get asked this every couple of months on a panel or by a journalist, generally in the face of current events that are clearly not going the way I want them to.

I have a stock answer: "So many people support me and believe in me. It makes it easy to do what I do. I have an incredible privilege in that I get to try to make good things happen in the world. And I'm now on a list of people who might be able to make them happen."

It's a very satisfactory answer. Appropriately uplifting and conciliatory. It's also generally true . . . up to a point.

You see, it was very true in 2020. I had cheering crowds of thousands and people urging me on in every situation. It was impossible *not* to want to kick ass and give it my all in that kind of environment. But now, it isn't like I'm running for president at every moment. There aren't crowds to see me pick up groceries for my kids. So what keeps me going?

A lot of it is the people I work with. I get reminded of what soldiers say about going back on a second tour of duty. How do they go back out given what they've seen? They may say something like, "It's not about the mission or even the country, it's about the people next to you in your unit. You don't want to let them down."

Random people on the street believe in me. But there are also those who have put their lives on hold or bet their careers on my ability to make good things happen. I see them every day. That makes it mandatory for me to get out there and do my best.

Another thing that keeps me going: I try to imagine young, angry, dislocated me seeing the position I'm in now. Young me would be awestruck by so many things about my life, particularly that I'm happily married with a loving family that actually wants to spend time with me. But also at the opportunities I have.

People reach out to me all the time asking for information or help with things. Sometimes on the street it's something to do with public policy, like "Why is my rent so high?" or "Why do I have to pay credit card fees when I shop?" And part of me is like, *What are you asking* me *for? I don't control anything. I'm just a dude you saw on TV.*

But then I reverse that. I'm well-known. I know people at the highest levels of power. I'm rich enough that I don't need to worry about keeping a roof over our heads on a monthly basis. I can get on TV anytime I want. I have a social media following in the seven figures. I have an organization.

One of the oddest things about this time in my life is that people will often come to me for my approval or buy-in or support. I have somehow become an establishment-type figure, despite being the consummate outsider all of my life and doing what I think is right regardless of prevailing opinion.

I spoke at Brown University, my alma mater, in February of 2025. I was invited by several student organizations. It was my first time back since the presidential campaign; I had Zoomed in for an event in 2020 but hadn't been back on campus.

I was honestly not sure what the reception would be. But it felt like the presidential campaign: the auditorium was filled to capacity with six hundred students and dozens more who were left outside. As soon as I came in the room, I was met with a wall of applause. I went around and high-fived dozens of students and took pictures with many of them afterward. A number of them told me that I made them feel better about the future. It was heartwarming, imagining myself in their shoes back when I was in college.

Miika, my old friend who was in a rock band in his twenties, said something to me a couple years ago that I took to heart: "Man, you are the most punk rock person I know." I took it as a high compliment.

What keeps me going? I still have more inside of me. I have music yet to play.

Chapter 49

Yangstradamus

Here are some of my predictions from past years:

"AI is going to come and eat our jobs."
—Me, 2018

"Eric Adams is corrupt."
—Me, 2021

"Running Joe Biden is a bad idea."
—Me, 2023

"I think we're going to get burritos."
—Me, 2026

Some of my predictions have aged well. Some, including sports predictions, not so much. Yet many people ask me for a sense of what's coming. Call me Yangstradamus.

So, since you've gone through the trouble of reading this book, I feel I owe you a picture of the near future, as I see it. What do I foresee? Is the future bright or bleak?

Before I get started, a quick story: A few years ago, CNN approached me about doing a TV show called *The Future of . . . with Andrew Yang*. The thought was that each episode I would go over the future of some industry or activity, like "The Future of Education" or "The Future of Transportation." It seemed interesting. I said I was open to it.

A few weeks later, the producers came back with an update: "Hey, Andrew, bad news. Americans don't like the future." They had run some audience surveys and focus groups, and what they discovered was that Americans found the future stressful and didn't want to think about it. "Good news: people like you; they just don't like being reminded about the future. We'll have to think of something else."

The way I see it is, the future is asymmetrical. There will be phenomenal advances, some of which will even touch the average person. But there will be a lot of changes that you probably won't like.

I meet with entrepreneurs, investors, and technologists in my spare time and get invited to fancy gatherings. We are going to see some crazy breakthroughs in areas like AI, biotech, quantum computing, and energy. A drug that simulates the effect of exercise in speeding up your metabolism and helping you lose weight? Yup. Computers that are so fast they can break every code and lead to new materials? On the way. Fusion reactors that will enable cheap, abundant energy? Sources say yes. AI that can code an app and a website for you based on your hopes and dreams? Sure. Your being able to remember which channel the game is on and how to log on? Nope.

So, if you're on the cutting edge, there are some tremendous developments on the horizon. But for the average person, things are going to suck for a while. There will be a ton of layoffs fueled by AI. I talked to the founder of a company—one you've heard of—who told me that he's looking to replace their two thousand customer service workers with AI. And this guy isn't some jerk—he looks a little like the Quaker Oats guy. Even the kindly uncle is going to be cutting workers this time.

Because of the stresses and desire to automate, we'll see more labor strikes. From longshoremen to teachers to nurses to baristas—everyone is going to be trying to get enough to keep it together. There will be protests. Think of us becoming a bit more like France, minus the croissants.

Young people in your lives will be dating AI girlfriends and boyfriends, like in the movie *Her*, but won't want to tell you about it. Hey, at least no one will get pregnant.

So, yes, things are going to suck for a while.

Do I have anything rosier for you? I'm a data guy, and this is what the data says. But if it makes you feel better, the data also says that following the decline, there will be a period of exhaustion, at which time people, tired of the conflict, will wonder, *Okay, what are we actually going to do in real life?*

That's where *we* come in.

I get asked about running for president all of the time. In a business setting I sometimes joke, "When do they give the Asian guy the CEO job? When no one else wants it." We are only a few years away.

Hunker down, build up, and take care of yourself and those around you. I'm sure folks in your life need you.

Oh, and comedians will become among the most trusted figures in America. I will have made the switch in the nick of time. See you at the club.

So speaketh Yangstradamus.

Chapter 50

$1,000

In early 2025, I had an epiphany.

The name of this book comes from what some people think when they see me. I'm the presidential candidate who wanted to give them money.

And it's true, I do. I think it's the best way to make things better for most people. My presidential campaign and I gave away $180,000, which is small change; we should have given away far more. Humanity Forward gave away $8 million during COVID. I lobbied for cash relief checks that put billions in people's hands when the economy shut down. I personally give away money all of the time; apparently, I'm AI's answer to "Which public figure is most likely to give you money?" That's something I'm very proud of.

But the scale is always off. See, there are 340 million Americans and the economy generates about $30 trillion. I want to ease poverty throughout the United States of America, which will require *billions*.

I consider myself a talented entrepreneur. There has to be a way.

Back in 2022, my friend Mark Cuban started Cost Plus Drugs, a company that buys generic drugs in bulk and then sells them back to the public at a modest 15 percent markup. This has the effect of saving Americans billions of dollars on drugs and also saves thousands of lives as people get medications they need. I thought to myself, *Mark is doing it right. Could I help lower Americans' costs in something else we all pay for every year?*

I made a list of the costs that keep us down: Housing. Healthcare. Food. Fuel. Our cell phones. Data, voice, and Internet. I could get us our cell phone data much cheaper! Americans spend about $300 billion a year on our cell phone services and data, or almost $1,000 per person annually. There's a lot of excess in there; the three big carriers—Verizon, AT&T, and T-Mobile—are paying shareholder dividends of over $20 billion per year and spending billions more in marketing. I was paying Verizon $140 a month for my own cell phone service. I know, I'm a chump.

In 2020, I campaigned on trying to make it so that we own our own data. Our data is now sold and resold by and to the tech companies for hundreds of billions of dollars a year. Could I get us all data and connectivity more cheaply, and then pledge not to use anyone's data for commercial gain? Of course, multiple discount wireless brands exist, but nine out of ten of us don't use them because they seem low-quality. We would need to build a different kind of brand. If I could get my own costs down to about $50 a month, I'd save myself over $1,000 a year. We could put people's savings in a high-yield savings account and help those funds to grow over time. We could introduce rewards for doing wholesome things like putting down your phone and using social media less.

There wasn't a values-based, good-guy wireless carrier in the US market at that time. I figured we could build one. What would we call it? We spitballed a bunch of names: Human Wireless. Purple. Noble Mobile.

Everyone loved Noble Mobile. Easy to spell, easy to remember, fun to say. So I visited the headquarters of one of the major carriers. Happily, some of the employees there were fans of mine. We went and hammered out a deal to license enough data to serve millions of customers.

Then we threw the no-phones Offline Party that drew hundreds of people in Manhattan in mid-2025. There was clearly a big appetite for a better relationship with our phones.

Now it was time to start entrepreneuring— staff up. Build a brand. Recruit spokespeople. Special recognition to Scott Galloway, who became the first investor and champion for Noble Mobile.

One morning we finally turned on the network

to test it. Then, a couple months ago, I switched from Verizon to Noble. It was weird; I'd had the same wireless provider for twenty-five years. How was it going to work? Would I notice any change?

I sat down and went through the switching process. It took about ten minutes. The icon on my phone changed from *Verizon* to *Noble*. It was still my phone. Still the same number. I started texting people and making phone calls. They were like, "Why are you calling?"

"No reason. Just making sure everything works."

It was the same phone experience. It was that easy. I genuinely felt freer. Maybe it was the fact that I had just gotten away from a vendor that I'd never loved, that I knew I had been overpaying but felt sort of beholden to. It turns out I didn't need them. I felt like Rocky at the end of *Rocky IV*: "If I can change, and you can change, everybody can change!"

I looked at the little savings wheel on my phone. It started out with $20 in potential data dividend for that month. The more I doomscrolled—which I am as guilty of as the next person—the less money I would get back at the end of the month. And any money I sock away starts earning 5.5 percent. My mobile plan would become a little savings account, as opposed to something I just threw money at each month. My savings would shoot up if I enlisted a friend.

By the time you read this, Noble Mobile will be up and running. Check it out if you want to be part of the consumer revolution in getting control of our own data, using our phones less, and keeping more of our own money. We want to improve your financial health, your mental health, and help you get out of the house more often. We are even looking to give early customers a way to benefit from the growth of the company.

We could improve the lives of millions of people.

The average American is spending about $83 a month on their data. If you pay $50 to Noble and get a $10 rebate for unused data every month, you would save about $500 a year, or $1,000 in two years, plus we would never sell or resell your data, we'd reward you for using your phone less, and we'd get you the highest interest rate possible.

One of the early adopters said, "I get it: you're trying to get us UBI on our phones."

$1,000. It's not every month, but it's a start. If this sounds appealing to you, go to noblemobile. com to check it out.

You see? I've been working on it this whole time.

Conclusion

Sometimes it happens when you least expect it. In July of 2025, I got a call from Liam deClive-Lowe, the head of Humanity Forward. If you remember, that's the wholesome advocacy org that I founded back in 2020 during COVID that has been trying to reduce poverty. Liam said, "Hey, I've got some great news. We met with dozens of legislators. Buried in the big beautiful bill were improvements to the child tax credit we've worked to get for years. Now, instead of dropping to $1,000 per child per year, the credit's going up to $2,200 per child per year—the expansion is permanent, and it's indexed to inflation."

He went on, "If Congress hadn't acted, it would've dropped from $2,000 per child back to just $1,000 by the end of the year. That would've increased child poverty nationwide. Now, there are no more artificial, politically designed cliffs that could hurt kids and families. No more slow erosion from inflation. And even if these changes aren't as good as some would want, they may come to find that these changes raise the floor of how helpful this benefit for children can be when they get the chance to build on it in the future. The net benefit to families is about $80 billion a year."

"Wow, thanks for telling me. Congratulations." I hung up the phone and looked at Evelyn. I said, "Well, it looks like we permanently improved life for millions of kids in the United States." That's what increasing the child tax credit would do for poor families—it would put more money in their hands each year. This money would push at least some out of poverty. The fact that it was passed in perpetuity means it is going to stick unless repealed.

It was the greatest achievement of my life. It was real. Sure, no one would know that it happened; there wouldn't be any press or fanfare. No one celebrates a lobbying victory. The families and kids who got to breathe a little bit better wouldn't know either.

But I would. *We* would.

Now you do too. If you donated to my presidential campaign, you helped make it happen. You helped make a lot of kids' lives just a little bit better. Buying this book also helped make some kids' lives better. *My* kids. Kidding!

Sometimes you win. Sometimes positive efforts pay off. They could be big or small. They can be the result of years of quiet work. Maybe it's your child doing something that shows that they were actually listening or watching.

As I've said, people frequently ask me what

259 ❖ Andrew Yang

I've been up to. Occasionally I'll say, "I'm an all-purpose do-gooder." I've realized that as a dad, CEO, movement leader, author, founder, husband, and influencer, my job is to pretty much show up every day and do the best I can. And that just about describes *everyone's* job. Show up and do the best we can. And then celebrate the moments and the wins, of any size.

A serial entrepreneur I have a lot of respect for said this to me: "It used to be that I was all about trying to measure the impact. But now, I believe you don't know what's going to touch or uplift someone. It's impossible to know. So now I just try to enjoy the process."

I'm not quite at that level. I'm constantly trying to put points on the board. But I'm learning. Learning to enjoy even the days when it's unclear whether anything moved an inch, because at least I was there. And most every day, some incredible people were right there with me.

Don't get me wrong, I still harbor big dreams. Some would call it a vision. I still think that poverty can be a thing of the past in the richest society in the history of the world. We could work three- or four-day workweeks, with AI doing untold work for us instead of replacing us. We could build an economy that serves human values and flourishing, instead of turning us all into servants to get kicked to the curb.

I even see a path from here to there. In a world

of numbers and data and money, can our humanity save us? I still hope so. It's the only thing we've got.

Thank you for rewarding my humanity these past years. I'm still working on it. I'll see you out there. It'll be great. Or at least entertaining. Let's go!

Acknowledgments

There are so many people to thank! First, thank you to *you*, for following me and believing in our capacity to change the world or even have a good time. It has been the honor of my life to work on your behalf, and I hope you know that I'm still tap-tap-tapping away for a brighter future. That tapping is the sound of me chiseling away at the wall for good things.

Thank you to my publisher, Johnny Temple; my agent, David Larabell of CAA; and Byrd Leavell of UTA, who made me an author in the first place.

Thank you to Evelyn, for being the best partner anyone could ask for, and to Christopher and Damian, for being Dad's amibros.

Thank you to Mom, Dad, and Larry for always being there, and to Theo, Marilyn, and Tony. We have to enjoy this time with your grandkids.

Thank you to Zach Graumann for making *Andrew Yang* a thing and betting your career on me all those years ago. I want to make the bet pay off in more ways than one!

Thanks to Jon Lou, Julian Low, Avery Kim,

and Daniel Fabelo for believing in the next chapter, and to Ethan Dunn, Ed McGlone, and Conrad Taylor for keeping us out of trouble.

Thanks to Miika Grady and Andy George for making growing up a lot easier.

Thank you to Liam deClive-Lowe for making the *Onion*'s words a reality.

Thanks to Dave and Elaine Chappelle for being awesome friends and helping me think I can make people laugh.

Thank you to Scott Galloway and Jonathan Haidt for being role models and voices of both reason and heart. You're what the country needs.

Thank you to Mark Cuban, Marc Lore, Kathryn Murdoch, Daniel Lubetzky, Jerry Yang, Peng Zhao, Jacqueline Novogratz, and Joe Tsai for the friendship and giving me goals to aspire to.

Thank you to Dean Phillips for laying it on the line.

Thank you to Nick Troiano, Rob Richie, Katherine Gehl, and Meredith Sumpter for thinking we can do better with this democracy of ours.

Thank you to Chris Anderson for inviting me to do a TED Talk! It was a lot of fun.

Thank you to Stephen Dubner for following where the story and the data lead.

Thank you to Matt Shinners, Lindsey Drath, Christie Todd Whitman, Kerry Healey, Michael Willner, Maryfrances Metrick, Keith Tom, Eric Grossman, Monika Andony, Spencer Reynolds,

Mario Arias, Carrie Ann Templeton, Forrest Kaplan, and the team at Forward, along with all who have supported us, including Daniel Fong, Kim Neal, Daryl Morey, Jeffery Lee, Peter Cooper, Deb Liu, David Liu, Joe Geraci, Dan Wisniewski, Ty Montague, Anthony DiPietro, and so many others too numerous to list here. History is proving us right.

Thank you for believing in Noble Mobile to Ethan Gottlieb, John Limotte, Michael Chatfield, Lily Salzman, Josh Targoff, Samer Hamadeh, Phil Schwarz, Sean Daley, Sara and Erin Foster, Michael Milstein, Kim Lee, Bradley Tusk, Greg and Sophia Gushee, Roy Yuan, Fabrice Grinda, Dan Kwon, Dan DiSalvio, Jason Kingdon, Ron Cao, Courtney Reum, Romeen Sheth, Phillip and Kristin Rapoport, Rich Rosenblum, Chok Oi, Jerry Tsong, Mike Borofksy, Jon Sposato, Josh Mohrer, Chaitanya Mehra, Keith Knee, Michael Chad Hoeppner, Enoch Liang, Lister Delgado, Mark Mao, Rajiv Kumar, Mat Farkash, Danny Warshay, Nihal Mehta, Jim and Anna McKelvey, Charlamagne, Cipha Sounds, Tim Urban, Andrew Fung, Derek Thompson, and again Scott Galloway. Why are we paying so much for data? It's time to Noble-ize people.

Christopher is right: I do have a lot of friends. I've missed so many names here. Thank you to anyone who has believed in me and our capacity to change things for the better.

#YangGangForever